NOSH

@NOSHBOOKS

EVERYDAY GLUTEN-FREE

by Joy May

& the family team

THE NOSH SERIES OF COOKBOOKS BY JOY MAY

ISBN: 9780993260964
ISBN: 9780956746450
ISBN: 9780956746498
ISBN: 9780993260919

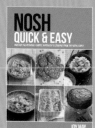
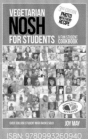

ISBN: 9780956746481
ISBN: 9780993260933
ISBN: 9780993260940
ISBN: 9780956746467
ISBN: 9780993260957

Contents

I have called this book "Everyday" because I wanted to create a book which has a permanent place on your work-top, ready to encourage you to try new recipes, even in the midst of busy days. Meals are simply put together and easy to present, giving great-looking food, suitable for any day of the week, as well as when friends are around.

I think, for those of us who eat gluten-free, the journey is becoming easier, with new 'free-from' ingredients popping up in the supermarkets each week. This gives us greater liberty in the things we can cook, without having to search high and low for our ingredients.

Even the appliance companies are trying to help us with gluten-free settings on their bread-makers. Great news for those wanting daily, fresh bread that doesn't cost the earth. For this reason, we have included a couple of great bread-maker recipes at the end of the book.

I hope that you will love this little book and that it becomes a part of your everyday gluten-free journey.

Why Gluten-free?

For those of us who are coeliac or gluten intolerant (like me) we probably already know the answer to 'why gluten-free?'. We want to avoid the painful side effects of consuming gluten from wheat, barley or rye — stomach cramps, sickness, bloating and even worse. Others may choose to eat gluten-free for additional health or fitness reasons.

There are many theories as to why gluten is causing the problems we are experiencing and why 'gluten-free' is becoming a necessity for many. No one can argue the fact that the problem appears to be increasing across the planet. Many researchers find compelling arguments suggesting that the root causes lie either in the significant modification of the wheatgerm itself, in order to increase yields, or the heavy pesticides and fertilisers applied to the crops, or the process used in the manufacture of the final product. Fundamentally, it would appear, we have created a problem which might not have existed before.

Consuming gluten when we are sensitive to it, can cause the lining of our guts to become inflamed, making it more difficult for our body to absorb nutrients. It is advisable to consult your doctor if you feel you need to eat 'gluten-free'.

Some gluten-free cooking can be reasonably straightforward, such as cutting out 'normal' glutenous flour, pasta, etc. and replacing it with gluten-free varieties. There are a few other things to look out for. I now carefully read the 'contents' labels of anything I buy in a jar or packet. This gluten-free journey has certainly introduced me to many new ingredients, such as polenta and quinoa, which I rarely used before, but which now feature in my recipes.

It is essential to build a store cupboard of good GF products. I also recommend making a weekly menu-plan before going to the supermarket (or ordering it online). This keeps cooking simple and efficient.

This is our MUG

If you have used NOSH books before, then you will be very familiar with 'our mug'. This mug is in all of our books. It holds ½ a pint or 300ml. A little while back, it sadly broke, so you can see the superglue holding it together! Alas, we don't use this exact mug to cook with anymore; there's only so many times a mug can be put back together ... a bit like Humpty Dumpty.

What is quicker than just grabbing a mug and filling it? What is easier to remember as a unit of measure than a 'mug of this', or 'two mugs of that'?

What could be simpler than a mug...?

ACTUAL SIZE

Why Sugar-free?

As you go through the book, you will see that we have not used any refined, processed sugar, but rather, replaced it with natural sweetness from ingredients such as raw honey, coconut sugar and pure maple syrup. This, of course, is not a requirement for eating gluten-free, but more part of our journey towards eating a much healthier and natural diet.

There is a current trend to 'demonise' sugar, but, of course, we need sugar as an energy source for our daily life and for extra bursts of activity. Thankfully, all vegetables provide us with some form of sugar, but generally, not the sweetness. If we want the sweetness which comes with sugar in a healthy form, then we need to consume it in its natural, wholesome state, as in the case of those ingredients we have already mentioned. Here, the sugar is 'packaged' naturally, together with water and amazing blends of natural nutrients such as vitamins, fibre, antioxidants and minerals. This 'packaging' means that we get wonderful health benefits, together with a controlled release of sugar into our system, rather than the 'sugar spikes', measured by a high Glycaemic Index (GI), which come from the processed stuff (typically 70 and above). Eating too much high GI food can contribute to heart disease, diabetes and obesity.

Using these 'natural sugars' produces delicious results. For instance, we used coconut sugar in a sticky toffee pudding which we tested in November. Everyone loved it so much, that we decided to make it part of our family, Christmas lunch.

If you want to go completely 'refined-sugar-free', as we do, then you will need to check food packets and jars, as things like stock, sauces, etc. will often have traces of sugar in them. Sometimes, the only way forward is to make your own sauces, which we have done in our book "NOSH Sugar-Free Gluten-Free".

Raw Honey

Raw honey is full of nutrients and enzymes, which are great for building up our immune system and fighting harmful bacteria. However, if it has been processed heavily, then it starts to fall into the same category as processed, refined sugar, with all of the accompanying dangers to health. This is why we choose RAW honey, which has not been pasteurised, or heavily filtered, thus, not losing any of its incredible health benefits. The result is that raw honey has a low GI of only 35-48 compared to regular honey, with a medium GI at 55-58.

Coconut Sugar

In some cultures, coconuts are almost worshipped for their incredible health benefits; indeed, every part of the coconut has its benefits. Coconut sugar comes from the flower of the coconut palm and has a final appearance very similar to fine brown sugar, but with none of the disadvantages, since brown sugar is processed as much as the white stuff. Coconut sugar provides the sweetness of sugar, but is high in magnesium and potassium and naturally provides B and C vitamins. It also has a low GI of only 35.

Pure Maple Syrup

Maple syrup is an excellent source of minerals. It includes manganese, which helps antioxidant defences, and riboflavin which helps the metabolic process. Generally, maple syrup is not heavily processed, but buying PURE maple syrup ensures that it meets the strict regulations adopted by the industry. Pure maple syrup has a GI of 54, still classed as low, but don't overdo it!

We understand that you may not want to go totally 'processed-sugar-free', especially if you have just started your gluten-free journey, but we do want to make this approach available to you. If you would rather not, then, to make these recipes work, you could replace the coconut sugar with light brown sugar, the raw honey with regular honey and the pure maple syrup with regular honey.

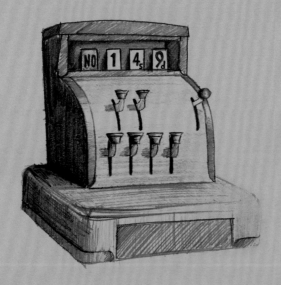

GF Buying Guide

Gluten-free foods are now readily available in supermarkets. Most of the ingredients in the book are available at the major supermarkets. However, some of them – chocolate ingredients, coconut sugar, nuts, maple syrup, raw honey – can be bought cheaper online. Raw honey is often available locally from beekeepers, or local butchers who sell their produce. I buy 450g jars of local raw honey from our butcher for £5. I find Healthy Supplies (online) very useful, because they have such a huge range of gluten-free ingredients. Amazon, of course, also has a good range at reasonable prices.

I do, regularly, shop online, as I am quite busy, and find it a great way to get all the foodstuffs I need. No trailing around looking for them!

So What Can We Eat?

 Okay

Gluten-free foods

- fresh fruit and veg.
- fresh meat and fish
- fresh dairy products
- fresh eggs
- spices and herbs
- peas, beans and lentils
- nuts and seeds
- sweetcorn
- rice: white, brown and wild
- tofu and soya
- sugar and honey
- pure oils
- rice flour
- buckwheat flour
- almond flour
- tapioca flour
- soy flour
- potato flour
- chickpea flour
- quinoa
- polenta
- cornflour

 Check the Label

These may have traces of gluten (you can buy GF versions of most of these)

- oats
- stock cubes (I use Kallo)
- corn tortillas and crisps
- cakes and biscuits
- burgers and sausages
- baking powder
- bicarbonate of soda
- suet
- curry pastes
- mustard and chutneys
- sweets and chocolate
- ice creams and desserts
- some roasted nuts
- ready-made foods
- some vinegars

❌ Avoid

These are generally full of gluten and you should avoid them

- wheat
- plain and self-raising flours
- couscous
- semolina
- spelt
- barley (in beer and malt extract)
- rye
- bulgar wheat
- cereals

BREAK-FAST

breakfast is always a tricky one
for us gluten-free folk

Pistachio Granola

Making your own granola is a great way to make sure you know exactly what you are eating. Bought breakfast cereals are a notoriously sneaky food stuff that often contain added sugar where you would least expect it.

90g **raw honey**

½ teaspoon **vanilla extract**

80ml **virgin coconut oil**

120g **pure maple syrup**

3 tablespoons **water**

1 tablespoon **tahini**

250g **GF oats**

100g **flaked almonds**

150g **pistachios**, roughly chopped

200g **coconut flakes**

50g **sesame seeds**

½ teaspoon **cinnamon**

1 Preheat the oven to 170°C fan oven/190°C/gas 5. Grease a large baking tray.

2 Put the honey, vanilla, coconut oil, maple syrup, water and tahini in a saucepan and gently heat.

3 Combine the rest of the ingredients in a large bowl, add the contents of the saucepan and mix well.

4 Pour onto the baking tray and spread out.

5 Place in the oven for 10 minutes. Take out of the oven and turn with a fish slice. Spread out the mixture again and return to the oven for a further 10 minutes.

6 Turn and stir again and leave to cool.

7 Place in a sealed container.

Why *pure* maple syrup?

Porridge

Nut Butter and Seeds

2 mugs **milk**

2 tablespoons **cashew nut butter**, see page 211

1 mug **GF oats**

2 tablespoons **pumpkin seeds**

4 tablespoons **pure maple syrup**

1 Put the milk and the cashew butter in a small saucepan and bring to the boil. Stir to make sure the nut butter is melted.

2 Add the oats and simmer for 2 minutes.

3 Divide between the bowls. Sprinkle over the seeds and drizzle over the maple syrup

---

Apple and Raspberry

1 mug **GF oats**

2 mugs **milk**

1 **Granny Smith's apple**, grated

1 mug **frozen raspberries**, defrosted

2 tablespoons **raw honey**

handful **flaked almonds**

1 Put the oats and milk in a small saucepan and bring to the boil. Simmer for 2 minutes.

2 Take off the heat and stir in the grated apple. Stir in the raspberries.

3 Divide between the bowls and drizzle with the honey. Sprinkle the almonds on top.

Banana and Hazelnut

2/3 mug **GF oats**

1/3 mug **oat bran**

2 mugs **milk**

2 **bananas**, sliced

4 tablespoons **maple syrup**

2 tablespoons **toasted, chopped hazelnuts**

1 Put the oats, bran and milk in a small saucepan. Bring to the boil and then simmer for 2 minutes.

2 Divide between the bowls, add the bananas on top and drizzle over with maple syrup. Sprinkle the hazelnuts on top.

Virgin Coconut and Blueberry

1/2 mug **GF oats**

1/2 mug **oat bran**

400ml tin **coconut milk**

2/3 mug **milk**

1 teaspoon **vanilla extract**

100g **blueberries**

runny raw honey

1 Put the oats, oat bran, coconut milk, milk and vanilla extract in a small saucepan and bring to the boil. Simmer for 2–3 minutes.

2 Divide between the bowls and add the blueberries. Drizzle over with the honey.

Chocolate Granola

BEN SAYS: "Every time dad makes Granola, we hear about how easy it was! It doesn't seem to matter how many times he has already told us, he tells us again. Needless to say, he's a big fan!"

100g **GF puffed brown rice**

100g **GF oats**

140g **coconut flakes**

50g **100% cocoa solids chocolate**, see page 210

80g **butter**

4 tablespoons **raw honey**

2 tablespoons **pure maple syrup**

2 tablespoons **water**

1 Preheat the oven to 170°C fan oven/190°C/gas 5. Grease a large baking tray.

2 Put the rice, oats and coconut flakes into a large bowl.

3 Put the rest of the ingredients into a small saucepan and gently heat.

4 Once everything is melted, pour into the dry ingredients and mix together thoroughly.

5 Spread out on the baking tray and place in the oven for 10 minutes. Remove from the oven and turn the ingredients over and spread out again. Return to the oven for a further 10 minutes.

6 Turn and stir again and leave to cool. Store in an airtight container.

7 Serve with milk, yoghurt, fruit etc.

Why *100%* cocoa solids chocolate?

See page 202 to understand our reasons

Eggs Benedict

TIM SAYS: "Ok, so this one might not quite be for every day (unless you are loaded), but this is certainly a lovely treat for a Saturday-morning breakfast. An absolute classic."

Sauce

100g **butter**

1 tablespoon **GF flour**

½ mug/150ml **milk**

1 **egg yolk**

½ teaspoon **lemon juice**

salt and **pepper**

2 slices **GF sourdough**

100g **smoked salmon**

2 **eggs**

1 teaspoon freshly-chopped **chives** (optional)

1 To make the sauce, on a gentle heat, melt the butter in a small saucepan and add the flour. Mix together and cook for 30 seconds. Add the milk and egg yolk and whisk together. Heat until the sauce begins to thicken. Add the lemon juice and season with salt and pepper.

2 Lightly toast the bread.

3 To poach the eggs, bring a frying pan of water to the boil and turn down to simmer very gently. Add the eggs, one at a time, and poach until the white has set.

4 Serve with the eggs and salmon on the toast, topped with the sauce and chives.

Bacon and Egg Hash

TIM SAYS: "In stark contrast to the refined Eggs Benedict on the previous page, this is a breakfast for when you are HUNGRY (and maybe not feeling quite so loaded). Guaranteed to fill you up and get you ready for the day."

3 medium **potatoes**, cut into 2cm cubes

1 tablespoon **olive oil**

200g **unsmoked, streaky bacon**

bunch **spring onions**, chopped

400g tin **cannelloni beans**, rinsed and drained

4 **eggs**

1 Put the potatoes in a pan of boiling water and simmer for 8 minutes. Drain and return to the pan.

2 Meanwhile, heat the oil in a large frying pan and fry the bacon until crisp. Remove from the pan and cut into 3cm pieces.

3 Add the onions, beans and potatoes to the frying pan and fry until things begin to brown a little.

4 Add the bacon back to the pan and stir gently.

5 Make 4 'holes' in the mixture and add the eggs. Continue to fry with a lid on the pan until the eggs are cooked. This should give time for some lovely crunchy bits to form on the bottom of the pan.

SNACKS

break free from boring sandwiches

Sausage Panzanella

JOY SAYS: "We always tease Ben about how 'picky' he was with food when he was younger (something he strongly protests against). So when he picked the olives out of this one, it just added 'fuel to the fire'."

2 tablespoons **olive oil**

4 slices **GF wholemeal bread**

1 tablespoon **paprika**

6 **GF sausages**

3 tablespoons **red wine vinegar**

3 tablespoons **olive oil**

1 teaspoon **raw honey**

20 **black olives**, halved

4 teaspoons **capers**, chopped

1 small **red onion**, thinly sliced

2 tablespoons freshly-chopped **basil**

250g **cherry tomatoes**, halved

50g **Parmesan cheese**, shaved

1 Heat the oil in a frying pan. Dip the bread on both sides to distribute the oil evenly. Fry on each side until golden. Remove from the pan and cut into croutons.

2 Place the paprika on a plate. Slit the sausage skins and remove. Squash the sausage into small pieces and roll them in the paprika.

3 Add another tablespoon of olive oil to the pan and fry the sausage pieces. Once cooked, take out of the pan and place in a large bowl.

4 Mix together the red wine vinegar, olive oil and honey.

5 Add to the bowl, along with the olives, capers, onion, basil, croutons, tomatoes and some of the Parmesan.

6 Divide between the plates and sprinkle the rest of the Parmesan over each plate.

Why *raw* honey?
See page 9 to understand our approach to sugar

£ 1.61 /PERSON · SERVES 4 · EASE ★★☆☆☆ · PREP 20 MINS

Spiced Lamburgers in Pitta

When you don't fancy a heavy burger in a bun, but you still want something with a bit of 'bite', why not give this a try?

Burgers

500g minced lamb
1 tablespoon **cumin**
1 tablespoon **coriander**
1 teaspoon **fennel seeds**
salt and **pepper**
egg yolk

1 tablespoon **olive oil** to fry
4 **GF pitta breads**

Slaw

Cos lettuce, thinly sliced
1/2 **cucumber**, grated
1 **red onion**, thinly sliced
1 **carrot**, grated

4 tablespoons **yoghurt**
2 tablespoons freshly-chopped **mint**

1 Mix together the burger ingredients. Divide into four and form the burgers.

2 Heat the oil in a frying pan and fry the burgers on a medium heat, until browned on each side and cooked through.

3 Mix together the 'slaw' ingredients.

4 Mix together the yoghurt and mint.

Butternut Fritters with Chive Dip

The combination of sweet, caramelised butternut squash and the freshness of the chive dip make this little snack a real winner.

1 medium **potato**

1/2 **butternut squash**, peeled

1/2 **onion**

1/2 teaspoon **salt**

1/2 teaspoon **pepper**

2 **eggs**

2 tablespoons freshly-chopped **basil**

3 tablespoons **GF SR flour**

olive oil to fry

Chive dip

3 tablespoons freshly-chopped **chives**

300ml **soured cream**

2 teaspoons **lemon juice**

2 tablespoons **mayo**

salt and **pepper**

1 bunch **spring onions**, chopped

1 Put the grater disc on a food processor and grate the potato, butternut squash, and onions. Use a normal grater, if you do not have a processor.

2 Mix together the salt, pepper, eggs, basil, and flour in a large bowl. Add all the grated veg and mix well.

3 Heat 2 tablespoons of oil in a large frying pan. The mixture will make 8 fritters, so make 4 at a time. Put the mixture in piles in the pan and then squash down. Fry on a medium heat, until browned on both sides.

4 Mix together the dip ingredients and serve with the fritters.

Baked Camembert with Red Onion Chutney

If baking Camembert is getting just a little 'passé' for you (if it is, then your life is great?!), why not 'turbo charge' it, by burying the Camembert in a sourdough loaf and covering it in red onion chutney?

GF sourdough loaf

250g **Camembert**

2 tablespoons **olive oil**

Red onion chutney

2 **red onions**, chopped

1 tablespoon **cider vinegar**

1 tablespoon **raw honey**

1 Preheat the oven to 200°C fan oven/180°C/gas 7.

2 Cut a hole in the top of the sourdough loaf the same size as the Camembert. Take the Camembert out of its packaging and place inside the loaf. Drizzle with oil and push a few rosemary sprigs into the Camembert.

3 Place in the oven for 20 minutes.

4 To make the chutney, heat the oil in a frying pan and fry the onions, on a medium heat, until they caramelise. This will take a while, but just keep stirring them. Add the cider vinegar and honey and cook for 1 minute.

5 Arrange everything on a platter and serve.

Why raw honey?

See page 9 to understand our approach to sugar

Smoked Mackerel Salad

RON SAYS: "Mackerel is a great source of Omega 3, which is wonderful for our hearts and immune system. Personally, I love fresh mackerel, but packets of smoked mackerel are so handy to have in the fridge ready for a dish like this one."

2 tablespoons **olive oil**

4 slices **GF bread**

Cos lettuce, sliced

½ **cucumber**, cut into sticks

200g **cherry tomatoes**, halved

265g packet **smoked mackerel**, skinned and flaked

Parmesan shavings

Dressing

4 tablespoons **mayo**

1 teaspoon **Dijon mustard**

1 teaspoon **Worcestershire sauce**

juice of a **lemon**

1 Heat the oil in a frying pan and fry the slices of bread. Remove from the pan and cut into croutons.

2 Mix together the lettuce, cucumber and tomatoes and stir in the croutons. Divide between four plates.

3 Divide the mackerel between the plates and sprinkle the Parmesan shavings on top.

4 Mix the dressing ingredients and drizzle over.

£ 1.42 /PERSON   SERVES 4   EASE ★☆☆☆☆   PREP 15 MINS   COOK 35 MINS

Pastrami Salad

We have only recently been using mixed carrots in our dishes and love them. They add such a great colour and really lift a simple salad into something special. If you can't find these funky coloured carrots, don't worry; it will work just fine with regular orange carrots.

4 **potatoes** cut into thin chips

3 tablespoons **virgin coconut oil**

Salad

4 medium **mixed carrots**, peeled and made into thin curls

bunch **spring onions**, sliced lengthways

100g **radishes**, sliced

½ mug **cashews**

Dressing

1 tablespoon **Dijon mustard**

juice of a **lemon**

4 tablespoons **extra virgin olive oil**

salt and **pepper**

150g **sliced pastrami**

1   Preheat the oven to 190°C fan oven /210°C/gas 7.

2   Put two tablespoons of coconut oil into a roasting tray and put in the oven for 5 minutes. Add the potato chips to the tin and mix into the oil. Spread out and season. Roast in the oven for 35 minutes.

3   Mix the salad ingredients.

4   Mix the dressing ingredients and add to the salad

5   Serve with the pastrami and chips

Why *virgin coconut* oil?
Not only can it taste great, but it has amazing health benefits too.

£1.21 /PERSON | SERVES 4 | EASE ★★★☆☆ | PREP 20 MINS | COOK 50 MINS | GRILL 5 MINS

Pancetta Potato Skins with Apple and Carrot Slaw

Ok, so we have used mixed carrots in two recipes in a row here. Don't worry, they are not in every recipe in the book! They work really well with a 'slaw', as the purple from the carrots bleed out and turns everything a great colour.

8 medium **potatoes**

77g **pancetta lardons**

1 mug grated **Gruyère cheese**

Apple and carrot slaw

2 **apples**, grated

3 **mixed carrots**, grated

1 bunch **spring onions**, chopped

4 tablespoons **yoghurt**

juice of a **lemon**

salt and **pepper**

1 Preheat the oven to 180°C fan oven/200°C/gas 6.

2 Prick each potato with a fork (so they don't explode in the oven). Bake in the oven for 50 minutes.

3 Mix together the 'slaw' ingredients and leave in the fridge until needed.

4 Take the potatoes out of the oven and cut each potato in half lengthways. Scoop out the middle, leaving about 5mm remaining in the skin.

5 Put the potato skins back on the roasting tray. Sprinkle over the cheese and then the pancetta lardons.

6 Place under the grill for about 5 minutes, or until the cheese begins to bubble.

7 Serve with the 'slaw'.

Smoked Haddock Omelette

BEN SAYS: "There is just something amazing about crinkle-cut chips. I don't know what it is, maybe it's to do with the increased surface that can crisp up. It could be that it's just a reminder of being a kid in the 80's. Oh yeah, that omelette was alright too..."

5 medium **potatoes**

2 tablespoons **olive oil**

20g **butter**

1 bunch **spring onions**, chopped

500g **smoked haddock**, cut into 2cm chunks

100g **spinach**, chopped

8 **eggs**, beaten + 1 tablespoon **water**

1 mug grated **Gruyère cheese**

1 Preheat the oven to 180°C fan oven/200°C/gas 6.

2 Cut the potatoes into thin chips. Place on a roasting tray and drizzle over the oil. Season with salt and pepper and mix everything together. Spread out and bake in the oven for 35–40 minutes.

3 Preheat the grill 20 minutes before the end of the cooking-time for the chips.

4 Put the butter in a large frying pan. Add the spring onions and fish and fry for 2–3 minutes, until the fish is almost cooked.

5 Add the spinach and allow it to wilt slightly.

6 Add the egg and water mixture. Allow to cook on the bottom of the pan and then move it slightly to allow the uncooked egg to touch the bottom of the pan.

7 While the egg is still a bit runny, sprinkle the cheese over the top and place under the grill. Cook until it is lightly browned.

Why use a *mug*?
See page 7 to see why we love mugs so much

Sourdough Toast with Chilli Pea Mash

RANDOM FACT: We found this plate in a little pottery in Bruges. Not all of our plates are this exotic (most of them are from charity shops or Tesco), so please excuse us for taking the opportunity to 'show off' a little with this one.

1½ mugs defrosted **frozen peas**

20g **butter**

½ **fat red chilli**

1 tablespoon freshly-chopped **mint**

2 tablespoons **virgin coconut oil**

2 slices **GF sourdough bread**

2 **eggs**

100g **soft goat's cheese**

1 Put the peas in a pan of boiling water and simmer for 1 minute. Drain and return to the pan along with the butter. Mash and then stir in the chilli and mint.

2 Heat the coconut oil in a frying pan. Add the bread and fry on both sides until lightly browned. Remove from the pan.

3 Add the eggs to the pan and fry until crispy around the edges and cook.

4 Spread the goat's cheese on the bread, top with the peas and eggs.

Why *virgin coconut* oil?

Not only can it taste great, but it has amazing health benefits too.

£ 1.62 /PERSON • SERVES 4 • EASE ★★☆☆☆ • PREP 15 MINS • V

Spinach and Broccoli Soup

There is a little twist to this recipe that you might not expect, in the form of the coconut milk and lemon. It really adds another dimension to this bright green soup.

1 tablespoon **olive oil**

2 cloves **garlic**, sliced

1 **onion**, sliced

2 tablespoons freshly-grated **ginger**

2 **parsnips**, chopped

1 **broccoli** cut into florets

1 mug **water**

1 **GF veg stock cube**

400ml tin **coconut milk**

200g **spinach**, chopped

juice of a **lemon**

4 slices **GF bread**

1 mug grated **Cheddar cheese**

1   Heat the oil in a large saucepan. Add the garlic, onions and ginger and fry for 2–3 minutes until the onion is softened.

2   Add the parsnips and broccoli, along with the water, stock cube and coconut milk. Bring to the boil and then simmer for 10 minutes.

3   Add the spinach and lemon juice. Simmer for 1 minute.

4   Blitz with a hand-held blender and reheat if necessary.

5   Toast the bread. Divide the cheese between the slices and toast under the grill until it bubbles and begins to brown. Slice into croutons.

Vegetable Soup with Pistou

After you have figured out how to say the name of this recipe without swearing, you might consider actually making it. In all seriousness, the dollops of pistou (similar to a pesto) add lovely little bursts of extra flavour.

2 tablespoons **olive oil**

1 **onion**, chopped

1 **leek**, sliced

200g **bacon lardons**

6 **tomatoes**, chopped

1 mug defrosted **frozen broad beans**

3 mugs **water**

1 **GF veg stock cube**

100g **green beans**, roughly chopped

100g **quinoa spaghetti**, broken up

Pistou

100g **fresh basil**

1 clove **garlic**

60g finely grated **Parmesan**

6 tablespoons **extra virgin olive oil**

1 Heat the olive oil in a large saucepan or wok.

2 Add the onions and leeks, fry until they begin to soften.

3 Add the bacon and fry until things begin to brown.

4 Add the rest of the ingredients and bring to the boil. Simmer for 10 minutes. Check to see if the spaghetti is cooked and, if not, simmer for a further 2–3 minutes.

5 Meanwhile, make the pistou. Put the ingredients in a blender (you can use a hand-held one). Whizz until everything is blended.

6 Serve the soup with dollops of the pistou.

Roast Butternut Squash Soup

Nut butter is an essential ingredient in this recipe, you can actually buy it in most supermarkets, but we have included a recipe in the back of the book to enable you to make your own. It is a really simple process, as long as you have a liquidizer or hand-held blender.

1 **butternut squash**, peeled and cut into 3cm chunks

1 **onion**, quartered

3 **carrots**, peeled and cut into chunks

1 tablespoon freshly-grated **ginger**

1 tablespoon **cumin**

3 tablespoons **olive oil**

4 mugs **water**

2 **GF veg stock cubes**

100g **nut butter**, see page 211

1 tablespoon **raw honey**

3 slices **GF bread**

1 Preheat the oven to 180°C fan oven/200°C/gas 6.

2 Put the vegetables on a large roasting tray. Add the ginger, cumin and olive oil. Season with salt and pepper. Squish everything around to mix it. Spread the veggies out.

3 Roast in the oven for 50 minutes.

4 Put the water, stock, nut butter and honey in a large saucepan. Bring to the boil and add the roasted veggies. Simmer for 5 minutes.

5 Blitz with a liquidizer or hand-held blender.

6 Toast the bread, cut into cubes and serve with the soup.

Why *raw* honey?

See page 9 to understand our approach to sugar

FAST

for when time is of the essence

Crispy Beef Noodles

200g **flat rice noodles**

Sauce

4 tablespoons **GF soy sauce**

2 tablespoons **mirin**

2 tablespoons **raw honey**

3 tablespoons **cornflour**

1½ mugs **water**

2 tablespoons **olive oil**

750g **beef mince**

2 teaspoons **paprika**

2 cloves **garlic**

2 tablespoons freshly-grated **ginger**

1 **savoy cabbage**, thinly sliced

200g **mangetout**, halved lengthways

1 bunch **spring onions**, sliced

2 tablespoons freshly-chopped **coriander**

1 In a large bowl, pour boiling water over the noodles and leave to stand for 10 minutes.

2 Put the sauce ingredients in a small pan and bring to the boil. The sauce should thicken.

3 Put the oil in a large frying pan and fry the mince until it is nicely browned. Add the paprika, garlic and ginger and fry for 2 more minutes, mixing well. Season well with salt and pepper.

4 Meanwhile, put the cabbage in a pan of boiling water and simmer for 3 minutes. Add the mangetout and simmer for 1 minute. Drain, return to the pan and add the spring onions and coriander. Mix.

5 Serve the rice noodles with the greens on top and then the meat. Drizzle over the sauce.

Why *raw* honey?

See page 9 to understand our approach to sugar

Chicken Korma with Coconut and Broccoli Rice

If you have never tried cooking rice with coconut milk, this a is great one to start with. We have also added chopped up broccoli. That means it cooks really quickly and adds another element to your rice.

1 mug **basmati rice**

400ml tin **coconut milk**

2/3 mug/200ml **water**

1 medium **broccoli**

1 tablespoon **olive oil**

1 large **onion**, sliced

3 **chicken breasts** cut into bite-size pieces

100g **mushrooms**, sliced

1 tablespoon **GF plain flour**

2 tablespoons **Korma curry paste**

1 mug **water**

1 **GF chicken stock cube**

1 Put the rice, coconut milk and water in a saucepan. Bring to the boil and then turn down to simmer, with a lid on, for 8 minutes.

2 Blitz the broccoli in a food processor (or chop very finely) and add to the pan. Simmer for a further 2 minutes. Stir together just before serving.

3 Meanwhile, heat the olive oil in a frying pan. Add the onions and fry until they begin to soften.

4 Add the chicken and fry until it is no longer pink on the outside.

5 Add the mushrooms and flour and fry for 1 minute.

6 Add the curry paste, water and stock cube and bring to the boil. Simmer for 3–4 minutes.

7 Serve with the broccoli rice.

Spiced Chicken with Cauliflower 'Couscous'

Tomato sauce

1 tablespoon **olive oil**

1 **onion**, chopped

1 clove **garlic**

3 **tomatoes**, chopped

1 tablespoon **raw honey**

1 tablespoon **cider vinegar**

2 tablespoons **tomato purée**

¼ mug **water**

3 **chicken breasts**, sliced

2 tablespoons **ras el hanout**

1 tablespoon **olive oil**

Cauliflower 'couscous'

1 large **cauliflower**

2 tablespoons **olive oil**

50g **pine nuts**

2 tablespoons freshly-chopped **parsley**

juice of a **lemon**

1 Heat the oil in a small saucepan and add the onion. Fry until it begins to soften.

2 Add the garlic and tomatoes, fry for a minute, add the rest of the sauce ingredients and bring to the boil. Simmer for 2 minutes and then blitz with a hand-held blender. Set to one side until needed.

3 Toss the chicken pieces in the ras el hanout and season with salt and pepper.

4 Heat the oil in the frying pan and add the chicken. Cook on a medium heat for 2–3 minutes, or until the pieces are cooked through.

5 Remove the stalk of the cauliflower and cut the rest into florets. Place in a food processor and blitz until you have something resembling breadcrumbs, (don't make it too fine). If you don't have a processor, just chop finely.

6 Heat the oil in a large frying pan, add the cauliflower and heat through on a medium heat, stirring frequently. Once the cauliflower begins to 'steam', it is cooked. Add the pine nuts, parsley and lemon juice and mix together.

7 Serve with the chicken and the sauce.

Why *raw* honey?

See page 9 to understand our approach to sugar

 £ 1.88 /PERSON SERVES 4 EASE ★★★☆☆ PREP 25 MINS

Crispy Noodle Cakes with Honey Chicken

Using coconut oil, especially for frying, is a great way of introducing flavour and also of getting the many health benefits derived from coconut. It's so good, some people even have a tablespoon of coconut oil each day!

300g pack **fresh, fine rice noodles**

2 **eggs**

1 tablespoon freshly-grated **ginger**

1/2 **fat red chilli**, thinly sliced

1/2 bunch **spring onions**, sliced

2 tablespoons **virgin coconut oil**

3 **chicken breasts**, cut into strips

2 tablespoons **GF soy sauce**

juice of a **lime**

2 tablespoons **raw honey**

200g **mangetout**, sliced

1 Mix together the noodles, eggs, ginger, chilli and onions.

2 Heat the coconut oil in a large frying pan. Divide the mixture into 4 and put two piles into the pan at a time, frying gently until browned on both sides. Repeat with the rest of the noodles.

3 Meanwhile, put the chicken, soy, lime and honey in a dish. Then transfer to a frying pan and cook gently for 6–8 minutes. The sauce should thicken to a lovely sticky 'goo'. Be careful not to burn the sauce.

4 Add the mangetout to a pan of boiling water and simmer for 1–2 minutes. Drain and serve with the chicken and noodles.

Crispy Bolognese Tortillas

Tired of your kids spraying spaghetti bolognese around their faces when they eat it? Possibly not, but here is a new 'spin' on the classic that is a bit of fun. The kids will enjoy watching the tortillas as they curl up under the grill (well at least Ben did).

1 tablespoon **olive oil**

1 **red onion**, sliced

6 **tomatoes**

1 tablespoons **GF soy sauce**

1 teaspoon **raw honey**

2 tablespoons **tomato purée**

1 **GF beef stock cube**

500g **beef mince**

6 **GF wraps**

2 mugs grated **Cheddar**

1 Preheat the grill.

2 Put the oil in a large frying pan, add the onions and fry until they are lightly browned.

3 Put the cooked onions, tomatoes, soy sauce, honey, tomato purée and beef stock cube in a food processor or liquidiser and blitz till smooth.

4 Add the beef to the frying pan and fry until lightly browned.

5 Add the sauce from the liquidiser. Season well with salt and pepper. Bring to the boil and simmer for 3–4 minutes.

6 Place the tortilla/wraps on baking trays and share the mixture between each tortilla. Sprinkle over the grated cheese and grill, on a low shelf, until the cheese melts and the edges of the tortillas are lightly browned.

Why *raw* honey?

See page 9 to understand our approach to sugar

Lamb Steaks with Cashew Nut Pasta

You don't have to worry about leaving lamb a little pink when you cook it (I think the pretentious terms is 'blushing'). If you can't quite handle the idea, you are more than welcome to cook it a little longer.

3 mugs **quinoa and rice pasta**

Sauce

2 tablespoons **raw honey**

bunch **spring onions**, chopped

2 tablespoons **toasted sesame oil**

3 tablespoons **cashew nut butter**, see page 211

2 tablespoons freshly-grated **ginger**

4 **leg lamb steaks**

2 tablespoons **toasted sesame oil** to fry

200g **sugar snaps**

1 Add the pasta to plenty of boiling, salted water and simmer until the pasta is tender.

2 Mix all the sauce ingredients and add 4 tablespoons of water from the pasta pan.

3 Heat the sesame oil in a frying pan. Season the lamb steaks with plenty of salt and pepper and fry on a fairly high heat for 3–4 minutes each side. Check that they are cooked to your liking; they can be eaten a little pink. Cook more on a medium heat if required. Remove from the pan and leave to rest.

4 Cook the sugar snaps in boiling water, simmer for 1 minute and then drain.

5 Drain the pasta, rinse in warm water and leave in the colander. Add the sauce to the pasta pan and heat through for about 30 seconds. Add the pasta back to the pan and mix together.

6 Serve the pasta with the sugar snaps on top and then the sliced lamb.

Prawn Moilee

This dish is originally from Kerala, a state in South India on the Malabar Coast, I am sure there are more authentic versions out there, but this one is delicious and so quick to make.

1 tablespoon **virgin coconut oil**

2 **onions**, chopped

3 cloves **garlic**, chopped

1 mug **rice**

2 teaspoons **turmeric**

2 tablespoons freshly-grated **ginger**

1 **fat red chilli**, chopped

1 **GF chicken stock cube**

400ml tin **coconut milk**

1 mug **water**

200g **mangetout**, sliced

juice of a **lemon**

500g **jumbo cooked prawns**

2 tablespoons freshly-chopped **chives**

2 tablespoons freshly-chopped **coriander**

1 Heat the coconut oil in a large frying pan or wok. Add the onions and garlic and fry for 1 minute.

2 Add the uncooked rice and cook for 30 seconds. Add the turmeric, ginger, chilli, stock cube, coconut milk and water and bring to the boil. Simmer with a lid on the pan for 9 minutes.

3 Add the mangetout, lemon and prawns and simmer with a lid on the pan for a further 2 minutes.

4 Stir in the chives and coriander and serve.

Why virgin coconut oil?
Not only can it taste great, but it has amazing health benefits too.

Pork Steaks with Fresh and Spicy Vegetables

2 mugs **GF pasta**

1 tablespoon **virgin coconut oil**

1 tablespoon **mustard powder**

4 **pork steaks**

1 tablespoon **virgin coconut oil**

1 tablespoon freshly-grated **ginger**

1 bunch **spring onions**. chopped

1 **red pepper**, roughly chopped

100g **sugar snaps**, halved

1 **pak choi**, sliced

1 **red chilli**, thinly sliced

250g **chestnut mushrooms**, sliced

juice of a **lime**

2 tablespoons **raw honey**

1 Add the pasta to plenty of boiling, salted water and simmer until the pasta is tender. Drain, rinse and return to the pan.

2 Meanwhile, heat the coconut oil in a frying pan. Rub the mustard and salt and pepper into the pork steaks and fry for 2 minutes each side on a high heat. Turn down the heat and fry gently until the steaks are cooked through. Depending on the thickness, you may need another 2 minutes each side. Set to one side to rest.

3 Heat the other tablespoon of coconut oil in a wok, add the ginger, spring onions and peppers, and fry for 1 minute.

4 Add the rest of the ingredients and cook for 1 minute.

5 Stir in the cooked pasta and season with salt and pepper.

6 Slice the pork steaks and serve on top of the pasta.

Why *raw* honey?

See page 9 to understand our approach to sugar

Pork and Parmesan Frikadellers

Frikadellers are a Danish meatball packed with flavour. Often they are a mixture of pork and veal, but we thought we would spare you having to buy veal and keep it simple.

Frikadeller

500g **pork mince**

1 mug/50g grated **Parmesan**

2 tablespoons **wholegrain mustard**

2 tablespoons freshly-chopped **basil**

1 **egg yolk**

Sauce

2 tablespoons **olive oil**

2 **red peppers**, chopped

6 **tomatoes**, roughly chopped

1 tablespoon **GF balsamic vinegar**

2 teaspoons **raw honey**

1 tablespoon **GF soy sauce**

300g **quinoa spaghetti**

1 Mix together the frikadeller ingredients and form into 12 meatballs.

2 Heat the oil in a large frying pan, add the peppers and fry until they begin to brown and soften. Add the tomatoes and fry for a further 5 minutes. Add the rest of the sauce ingredients and cook for a further 2 minutes. Pour into a processor and blitz, or use a hand-held blender

3 Add the spaghetti to plenty of boiling, salted water and simmer until tender. Drain, rinse and return to the pan.

4 Meanwhile, heat another 2 tablespoons of oil in a clean frying pan and fry the frikadeller until it is browned and cooked through.

5 Mix the sauce with the spaghetti. Serve with the frikadeller.

Crabcakes with 80's Crinkle-Cut Chips

You do not have to sprinkle the salad all over your table like Tim and Ben have done here. They just thought it would look fun, this is not, I repeat *not*, a serving suggestion!

6 medium **potatoes**

2 tablespoons **olive oil**

Sauce

6 tablespoons **mayo**

juice of ½ **lemon**

1 tablespoon **raw honey**

4 tablespoons **GF SR flour**

1 tablespoon **crème fraîche**

1 **egg**

zest of a **lemon**

1 tablespoon freshly-chopped **chives**

2 x 170g tins **shredded, crab meat**, drained

2 tablespoons **virgin coconut oil**

bag **green salad**

1 Cut the potatoes into thin chips. Place on a roasting tray and drizzle with olive oil. Season with salt and pepper, mix everything together and place in the oven for 30 minutes.

2 Meanwhile, mix together the sauce ingredients.

3 Mix together the flour, crème fraîche, egg, lemon zest and chives until smooth. Add the drained crabmeat and season with salt and pepper.

4 5 minutes before the end of the cooking-time for the chips, heat the coconut oil in a large frying pan. Drop dessertspoons of the crab mixture into the pan, and fry gently until lightly browned on both sides.

5 Serve together with the chips, salad and sauce.

Chicken Schnitzel with Mustard Sauce

6 medium **potatoes** cut into wedges

2 tablespoons **olive oil**

Sauce

200ml **double cream**

2 teaspoons **Dijon mustard**

juice of ½ **lemon**

½ teaspoon **cumin**

½ teaspoon **ground coriander**

½ teaspoon **cinnamon**

4 slices **GF brown bread**, made into breadcrumbs

1 **egg**

3 **chicken breasts**

2 tablespoons **toasted sesame oil**

1 tablespoon freshly-chopped **basil** to garnish, (optional)

1 Preheat the oven to 180°C fan oven/200°C/gas 6. Put the potato wedges on a large roasting tray. Pour over the oil, season well with salt and pepper, and mix everything together. Spread the wedges out and roast in the oven for 45 minutes.

2 Mix together the sauce ingredients.

3 Mix the spices with the breadcrumbs and season well with salt and pepper.

4 Beat the egg and put in a bowl.

5 Put the chicken breasts between cling film and bash with a rolling pin until they are about 1cm thick.

6 10 minutes before the wedges are cooked, heat the oil in a frying pan.

7 Dip the chicken breasts in the egg and then press into the breadcrumbs.

8 Fry gently for about 2 minutes per side. You may need to cook in batches if your frying pan is not big enough.

9 Cut the chicken into strips and serve.

£ 1.49 /PERSON — SERVES 4 — EASE ★★☆☆☆ — PREP 15 MINS — COOK 20 MINS

One-Pot Pork and Apple Bake

Removing the lid for the final ten minutes of the cooking-time allows the bits on top to go nice and crispy.

2 tablespoons **olive oil**

1 **red onion**, sliced

200g **bacon**, cut into chunks

500g **pork mince**

1 **red apple**, cut into small chunks

250g **mushrooms**, sliced

1 mug **basmati rice**

2 mugs **water**

1 **GF veg stock cube**

2 tablespoons **sun-dried tomato purée**

2 tablespoons freshly-chopped **basil**

1 Preheat the oven to 180°C fan oven/200°C/gas 6.

2 Heat the oil in a hob-to-oven casserole dish. Add the onion and fry for 2 minutes. Add the bacon and fry for another 2 minutes.

3 Add the mince, season well with salt and pepper and fry until the meat is no longer pink.

4 Add the apple, mushrooms, rice, water, stock cube and tomato purée. Mix together well and bring to the boil.

5 Stir in the basil.

6 Put a lid on the pan and bake in the oven for 10 minutes. Remove the lid and cook for a further 10 minutes.

Why use a *mug*?
See page 7 to see why we love mugs so much

Flaked Cod with Broccoli Rice

25g **butter**

1 **red onion**, sliced

1 **orange pepper**, cut into chunks

1 mug **basmati rice**

2 mugs **water**

1 **GF fish stock cube**

1 head **broccoli**, main stalk removed and cut into florets

4 pieces **cod**, cut into bite-sized pieces

1 mug grated **Parmesan**

3 tablespoons freshly-chopped **coriander**

1 Heat the butter in a frying pan, add the onion and pepper and fry until they begin to soften. Season well with salt and pepper.

2 Add the rice and allow it to absorb the juices from the pan.

3 Add the water and stock and cook gently for 7 minutes with a lid on the pan.

4 Blitz the broccoli in a food processor. Add to the rice and cook for 3 minutes with the lid on the pan.

5 Add the fish and cook, with a lid on the pan, for 2 minutes, or until the fish is no longer opaque. Add a little more water if the pan gets dry.

6 Take off the heat and add the Parmesan and coriander. Stir gently and serve.

£ 1.46 /PERSON — SERVES 4 — EASE ★★★★☆ — PREP 25 MINS

Five-Spice and Sesame Chicken

You could be forgiven for thinking we have burnt this, but actually the combination of the five-spice and the honey will give you this colour. You do need to be careful when frying though, as the five-spice can still be easily burnt.

³/₄ mug **basmati rice**

1 teaspoon **turmeric**

1 **broccoli**

100g **sugar snaps**

160g tin **sweetcorn**

1 **fat red chilli** cut into rings (optional)

3 **chicken breasts**, cut in ½ horizontally,

2 teaspoons **Chinese 5 spice**

2 tablespoons **sesame seeds**

juice of a **lemon**

1 tablespoon **runny raw honey**

1   Put the rice in a saucepan with 1½ mugs of boiling water and add the turmeric. Simmer with a lid on for 8 minutes.

2   Blitz the heads of the broccoli in a processor. Add the broccoli and simmer for a further 2 minutes.

3   Add the sugar snaps, sweetcorn and chilli and stir together.

4   Meanwhile, toss the chicken pieces in the 5 spice and sesame seeds.

5   Heat the oil in a large frying pan and cook the chicken on a medium heat, until browned on each side and cooked through. Drizzle the lemon and honey over the chicken and then cut into smaller strips, see photo.

6   Serve with the rice.

Why *raw* honey?

See page 9 to understand our approach to sugar

Lamb Pilaf with Wild Rice

We are really enjoying using wild rice in our recipes at the moment, it takes much longer to cook than 'normal' rice, but it adds a real nuttiness and bite to a dish. Here we have chosen Camargue rice, which is a red rice from the Camargue region of Southern France.

3 tablespoons **olive oil**

1 **onion**, sliced

500g **lamb mince**

2 tablespoons **cumin**

2 tablespoons **coriander**

1 teaspoon **turmeric**

2 tablespoons freshly-grated **ginger**

2 cloves **garlic**, finely chopped

1 mug **Camargue rice**

2 mugs **water**

1 **GF veg stock cube**

4 tablespoons **pine nuts**

1/3 mug **ready-to-eat dried apricots**

100g **spinach**, roughly chopped

1 Preheat the oven to 180°C fan oven/200°C/gas 6.

2 Heat the oil in a hob-to-oven casserole dish. Add the onions and fry until they begin to brown. Add the lamb and cook until it is no longer pink on the outside.

3 Add the spices, ginger and garlic and cook for 1 minute.

4 Add the rice and cook for 1 minute.

5 Add the water, stock cube, pine nuts and apricots. Bring to the boil. Place in the oven, with a lid on the pan, for 40 minutes.

6 Remove from the oven and stir in the spinach.

Harissa Salmon

Harissa is a spicy and aromatic chilli paste, widely used as a staple in Middle Eastern and North African cooking. It adds a real kick of spice to any dish.

4 **salmon steaks,** preferably skin left on

1 tablespoon **harissa paste**

1 tablespoon **olive oil**

Sauce

4 tablespoons **Greek yoghurt**

1 teaspoon **raw runny honey**

juice of a **lemon**

pinch **saffron**

1 tablespoon **virgin coconut oil**

1 **cauliflower**

zest of a **lemon**

6 **ready-to-eat dried apricots**, chopped

3 tablespoons freshly-chopped **coriander**

1 Marinate the salmon steaks in the harissa paste for 10 minutes.

2 Mix the sauce ingredients together.

3 Break the cauliflower up into florets and blitz in a food processor until it resembles breadcrumbs.

4 Heat the coconut oil in a large frying pan and fry the cauliflower for 2–3 minutes. Add the rest of the ingredients and fry for a further 2 minutes, stirring frequently.

5 Heat a tablespoon of olive oil in a frying pan and fry the salmon on a medium heat until nicely browned on both sides and cooked through.

6 Serve with the cauliflower mixture and the sauce.

Why virgin coconut oil?

Not only can it taste great, but it has amazing health benefits too.

Chicken and Mango Rice Salad

3 **chicken breasts**, cut into strips

zest and juice of a **lime**

2 teaspoons **garam masala**

50g **desiccated coconut**

3/4 mug **basmati rice**

2 tablespoons **toasted sesame oil**

1 **fresh mango**, cut into small cubes

1 bunch **spring onions**, chopped

1/2 **fat red chilli**, finely chopped

3 tablespoons freshly-chopped **coriander**

Dressing

150ml **natural yoghurt**

juice of 1/2 **lime**

1/3 **cucumber**, grated

1 Put the chicken breast to marinate in the lime juice and zest.

2 Mix together the garam masala and coconut and season well with salt and pepper.

3 Add the rice to a saucepan with 1½ mugs of boiling water. Bring to the boil and simmer with a lid on the pan for 10 minutes..

4 Heat the sesame oil in a large frying pan. Dip each piece of chicken in the coconut mixture. Fry in the pan over a medium heat, taking care not to burn the coconut. Fry until nicely browned and cooked through.

5 Mix together the rice, mango, spring onions, chilli and coriander.

6 Mix together the dressing ingredients and serve everything together.

SUPER
SIMPLE

for those times when you really
don't want to think too much

Rump Steak with Pesto Spaghetti

TIM SAYS: "Ok, so *I* cooked this one and I am sure you can tell that I like my steak rare! We do this a lot in this book. You are more than welcome to cook your steak for longer, but we think it looks great contrasting against the green spaghetti."

300g **quinoa spaghetti**

Pesto

½ clove **garlic**

100g fresh **basil**

½ mug **pine nuts**

½ mug finely-grated **Parmesan**

4 tablespoons **extra virgin olive oil**

2 tablespoons **olive oil**

3 pieces **rump steak**

1 Put the spaghetti in a large pan of boiling, salted water and simmer for 10 minutes. Take out ½ mug of water for the pesto and drain the rest. Rinse with warm water and leave in the colander.

2 Put the pesto ingredients in a liquidiser or processor and blitz. When the spaghetti is cooked, add the ½ mug of pasta water and give it another quick whizz.

3 Heat the oil in a large frying pan. Add the steak, season well with salt and pepper and fry on each side for 2 minutes. This will give you a rare steak. Cook for longer on a medium heat if you like the steak less rare. Take out of the pan and cut into pieces.

4 Add the pesto to the spaghetti pan and heat through. Add the spaghetti and mix together.

5 Serve with the steak.

Why use a *mug*?
See page 7 to see why we love mugs so much

Grilled Salmon and New Potatoes

This is one of those dishes that looks great when you bring it to the table in the dish it was cooked in. Everyone grabbing what they want from the middle of the table is always fun.

700g **new potatoes**, halved

20g **butter**

1 tablespoon **olive oil**

4 **salmon fillets**

bunch **spring onions**, sliced

150g **soured cream**

juice of a **lemon**

2 tablespoons freshly-chopped **chives**

100g **Gruyère cheese**, grated

1 Put the potatoes in a pan of boiling, salted water, simmer for 10 minutes and drain. Return to the pan, with the butter, and mix together.

2 Meanwhile, heat the olive oil in a frying pan. Add the salmon fillets, skin side down, and fry until they are cooked halfway up the fillet. You will see the fish changing colour. Add the spring onions to the pan and take off the heat.

3 Preheat the grill.

4 Tip the potatoes into a casserole dish. Place the salmon on top. Spread the soured cream over and drizzle the juice over the fish. Add the chives.

5 Top with the cheese and place under the grill until the cheese begins to bubble and brown.

£ 1.07 /PERSON

SERVES 4

EASE ★★☆☆☆

PREP 15 MINS

Spaghetti Carbonara

We have said this one takes 15 minutes, but actually, you can pretty easily make it in just over the amount of time it takes to cook the spaghetti. Perfect for those days when you are tight on time.

300g **quinoa spaghetti**

1 mug defrosted **frozen peas**

300g **streaky bacon**

1 clove **garlic**, chopped

1 **fat red chilli**, chopped

2 **egg yolks**

200ml **crème fraîche**

juice of ½ **lemon**

Parmesan to serve

1 Put the spaghetti in a large pan of boiling, salted water and simmer for 9 minutes. Add the peas and simmer for one more minute. Drain and rinse under hot water and return to the pan.

2 Meanwhile, fry the bacon until nicely browned and crisp. Take out of the pan and cut into small pieces.

3 Fry the garlic and chilli for 30 seconds.

4 Beat together the egg yolks, crème fraîche and the lemon. Stir into the spaghetti, along with the bacon, chilli and garlic.

5 Stir together and serve with some grated Parmesan on top.

£2.68 /PERSON | SERVES 6 | EASE ★☆☆☆☆ | PREP 20 MINS

Normandy Fish Stew

We had this for the first time when we were on our annual family holiday with the whole gang (with all the kids, there were 11 of us in total) cooking out of a tiny kitchen in France. We were determined to be as authentically French as possible with every meal, just for fun. This was a gem of a meal and too good not to make the cut for this book.

50g **butter**

bunch **spring onions**, sliced

1 **leek**, sliced

2 **celery sticks**, sliced

250g **chestnut mushrooms**, sliced

500ml **cider**

300ml **double cream**

400g **cooked prawns**

2 **salmon fillets**, cut into bite-sized pieces

2 **cod fillets**, cut into bite-sized pieces

3 tablespoons freshly-chopped **parsley**

GF crusty bread to serve

1 Heat the butter in a large pan or wok.

2 Add the spring onions, leeks and celery and fry for 1 minute.

3 Add the mushrooms and fry for 2 minutes.

4 Add the cider and cream and bring to the boil.

5 Add all the fish and bring to the boil. Simmer for 2 minutes and then check to see everything is cooked.

6 Stir in the fresh parsley and serve with the crusty bread.

Saffron Noodles with Paprika Chicken

Adding saffron to a dish is guaranteed to transform it. In this case it transforms the noodles into these bright, yellow ribbons of tastiness. Don't go crazy with the saffron though, you can have too much of a good thing. Plus, some say, it's more expensive than gold.

200g **ribbon rice noodles**

pinch **saffron**

3 **pak choi**, sliced

Sauce

2 tablespoons **nut butter**, see page 211

1 tablespoon **cornflour**

2 tablespoons **GF soy sauce**

2 tablespoons **GF fish sauce**

juice of a **lime**

bunch **spring onions**, sliced

3 **chicken breasts**, cut into bite-sized pieces

2 teaspoons **cumin**

2 teaspoons **coriander**

1 teaspoon **smoked paprika**

2 tablespoons **toasted sesame oil**

2 tablespoons freshly-chopped **coriander**

1 Put the rice noodles in a large bowl with enough boiling water to cover them. Add the saffron and mix in. Leave to stand for 9 minutes.

2 Add the pak choi and mix together a little, so the pak choi is below the water. Leave for 1 minute and then drain.

3 Meanwhile mix together the sauce ingredients.

4 Put the chicken pieces in a bowl and add the cumin, coriander and paprika. Mix together.

5 Heat the sesame oil in a frying pan and add the chicken. Cook for 3–4 minutes, turning the chicken to make sure it cooks evenly. Remove from the pan and set to one side.

6 Add the sauce to the pan and heat for 1 minute; the sauce should thicken.

7 Serve with the coriander sprinkled over.

£ 1.20 /PERSON · SERVES 4 · EASE ★☆☆☆☆ · PREP 25 MINS

Tabbouleh with Smoked Mackerel

Original versions of this come from Lebanon and would typically be packed with far more parsley than we have included here. Often served as a side dish as part of a larger meal. We have gone with the simple addition of some mackerel to convert it into a hearty meal in its own right.

100g **buckwheat**

2 tablespoons freshly-chopped **parsley**

2 tablespoons freshly-chopped **mint**

1 **red onion**, finely chopped

100g **cherry tomatoes**, halved

1 tablespoon **cider vinegar**

1 teaspoon **paprika**

1 teaspoon **cumin**

1 tablespoon **pure maple syrup**

2 tablespoons **extra virgin olive oil**

250g packet **cooked, peppered mackerel**

1 Put the buckwheat in a pan of boiling water and simmer for 20 minutes. Drain and rinse with cold water.

2 Mix together the rest of the ingredients, apart from the mackerel.

3 Divide between the plates and flake the mackerel on the top.

Italian Tuna and Olive Pasta

Before dismissing this recipe as just another tuna pasta dish, try it first. We have opted for using jarred tuna instead of tinned, which comes out a little more expensive (although, still not as expensive as fresh tuna steaks). These chunky flakes have a much fresher flavour and are a great, little upgrade.

3 mugs **rice and quinoa pasta**

220g jar **tuna in olive oil**

1 bunch **spring onions**, chopped

1 clove **garlic**, chopped

400g **cherry tomatoes**, halved

2 tablespoons freshly-chopped **basil**

10 **green olives**, roughly chopped

1　Add the pasta to plenty of boiling, salted water and simmer until the pasta is tender. Drain, rinse and return to the pan.

2　Meanwhile, pour about 2 tablespoons of the oil from the jar of tuna into a wok, or large frying pan. Add the onions, garlic and tomatoes and fry for about 5 minutes or until the tomatoes begin to fall apart. Season with salt and pepper.

3　Break up the tuna a little and add to the wok.

4　Drain the pasta and add to the wok along with the basil and olives and serve.

Sweet and Sour Pork Noodles

200g **rice noodles**

200g **sugar snaps**, sliced lengthways

1 tablespoon **olive oil**

4 **pork steaks**

Sweet and sour sauce

1 mug **water**

2 tablespoons **tomato purée**

2 tablespoons **cider vinegar**

1 tablespoon **GF soy sauce**

2 tablespoons **pure maple syrup**

1 tablespoon **cornflour**

1 bunch **spring onions**, sliced

1   Put the rice noodles in a large bowl and cover with boiling water. Leave to stand for 9 minutes. Add the sugar snaps and leave for another minute. Drain.

2   Heat the oil in a frying pan and add the pork steaks. Fry on a high heat for 2 minutes each side. Fry for a further 3–4 minutes each side, with a lid on the pan. Make sure the pork is cooked through. Remove from the pan and cut into bite-sized pieces.

3   Meanwhile, mix together the sauce ingredients.

4   Add the sauce to the pan and bring to the boil. The sauce should thicken.

5   Serve with the drained noodles and the sauce over the pork.

Why *pure* maple syrup?
See page 9 to understand our approach to sugar

Mushroom and Pancetta Risotto

TIM SAYS: "This will technically serve four 'normal' people, so feel free to follow this recipe as it is. In my house, however, this would typically be devoured almost entirely by just me and my wife, it is *that* 'moreish'".

1½ mugs **basmati rice**

½ teaspoon **turmeric**

25g **butter**

1 tablespoon **olive oil**

2 **onions**, sliced

350g **pancetta lardons**

250g **mushrooms**, sliced

½ teaspoon **cumin seeds**

juice of a **lemon**

1 Put the rice in a saucepan with 3 mugs of boiling water and the turmeric. Simmer for 10 minutes, with a lid on the pan. The water should be absorbed by the end of the cooking-time.

2 Meanwhile, melt the butter and oil in a large frying pan and fry the onions and pancetta lardons until they begin to brown. Season well with salt and pepper.

3 Add the mushrooms and cumin seeds and cook for 2-3 minutes.

4 Stir in the lemon juice.

5 Mix in the cooked rice and serve.

Why use a *mug*?

See page 7 to see why we love mugs so much

Spanish Fish Salad

2 tablespoons **olive oil**

2 **small red peppers**

3 cloves **garlic**, sliced

3 slices **GF bread**

2 tablespoons **toasted hazelnuts**

2 tablespoons **toasted flaked almonds**

½ **red onion**, thinly sliced

2 tablespoons freshly-chopped **parsley**

16 **black olives**, halved

160g tin **tuna**

Dressing

1 tablespoon **cider vinegar**

2 tablespoons **extra virgin olive oil**

1 tablespoon **raw honey**

1 **Cos lettuce**, sliced

8 **anchovies**

300g **cooked herring**, cut into bite-sized pieces

1 Heat the oil in a large frying pan, add the peppers and garlic and fry until they begin to brown. Remove from the pan and place in a large mixing bowl.

2 Add a little more oil and fry the bread until browned on both sides. Remove from the pan and cut into croutons. Set to one side.

3 Add the hazelnuts, almonds, parsley, onions, olives and flaked tuna to the bowl and gently mix.

4 Mix together the dressing ingredients, add to the bowl and gently stir.

5 Divide the lettuce and the contents of the bowl between the plates. Sprinkle over the croutons, herring and anchovies.

Salmon and Rice Salad

3/4 mug **basmati rice**

1 teaspoon **turmeric**

1 tablespoon **olive oil**

4 pieces **salmon steak**

100g **feta cheese**

bunch **spring onions**, sliced

1/2 mug **pine nuts**

1 **Little Gem lettuce**, sliced, to serve

2 tablespoons freshly-chopped **chives**

Dressing

juice of a **lemon**

1 tablespoon **raw honey**

2 tablespoons **extra virgin olive oil**

1 teaspoon **wholegrain mustard**

salt and **pepper**

1 In a small saucepan, add the rice and turmeric to 1½ mugs of boiling water. Bring to the boil and then turn down to simmer, with a lid on the pan, for 10 minutes. Allow to cool a little.

2 Meanwhile, heat the tablespoon of olive oil in a small frying pan. Add the salmon, season with salt and pepper and fry gently on each side for 2–3 minutes. Set to one side until needed.

3 Mix together the cooled rice, crumbled feta, spring onions, pine nuts and lettuce.

4 Top with the salmon and chopped chives. Combine the dressing ingredients and pour over each serving.

£2.00 /PERSON — SERVES 4 — EASE ★★☆☆☆ — PREP 15 MINS

Chorizo Spaghetti

We find that rinsing the quinoa pasta with warm water, after cooking it, makes a big difference to how sticky it gets. This is especially true if you need to leave it sitting for a minute or so.

300g **quinoa spaghetti**

1 tablespoon **olive oil**

240g **chorizo,** chopped

6 **tomatoes**

1 **onion,** cut into 4

½ mug **water**

1 teaspoon **cornflour**

1 **GF beef stock cube**

2 tablespoons **sun-dried tomato purée**

25g fresh **basil**

1 Put the spaghetti in a large pan of boiling, salted water and simmer for 10 minutes. Rinse with warm water and leave in the colander.

2 Heat the oil in a large frying pan and fry the chorizo for 2–3 minutes.

3 Put the tomatoes, onion, cornflour, water, stock cube, tomato purée and basil in a blender and blitz.

4 Add the sauce to the chorizo and simmer for 4–5 minutes.

5 Add the chorizo mixture to the pasta and combine.

Warm Steak Salad with Pistachio Dip

TIM SAYS: "I might have pushed the limits a little too far when it came to how rare I cooked the steak in this one, but it tasted great. I had the pan really hot so the outside was lovely and browned. I won't be offended if you follow the instructions below to get a slightly more well-done steak."

Pistachio dip

100g **pistachios**

3 tablespoons **extra virgin olive oil**

200g **feta cheese**

2 tablespoons freshly-chopped **basil**

100ml **Greek yoghurt**

juice of a **lemon**

1 tablespoon **virgin coconut oil**

3 **rump steaks**

Warm Salad

200g **sprouting broccoli**

½ **savoy cabbage**

1 mug defrosted **frozen peas**

25g **butter**

12 **olives**, chopped

4 **sundried tomatoes**, chopped

1 **fat red chilli**, chopped

1 Put the pistachios in a food processor and pulse a few times. Add the rest of the dip ingredients and pulse a few more times. Set to one side until needed.

2 Heat the coconut oil in a frying pan, season the steaks well with salt and pepper and fry for 2 minutes each side on a high heat. Turn down the heat and fry for another 2 minutes each side. Cook longer if you like your steak well done. Leave for a couple of minutes and then slice into strips.

3 While the steak is cooking, put the broccoli and cabbage in a pan of boiling water and simmer for 3 minutes.

4 Add the defrosted peas and simmer for a further 1 minute. Drain and return to the pan. Add the rest of the salad ingredients and gently mix.

5 Serve with the steak and dip.

Why *virgin coconut* oil?

Not only can it taste great, but it has amazing health benefits too.

Seafood Curry

BEN'S CHILLI TIP: "When deseeding chillies, you need to remember that it is, in fact, the flesh holding the seeds in place that contains most of the heat, so be careful to remove that too, if you don't want things to be too spicy. However, if you fancy a kick, leave the seeds and everything in and cook for a little longer at stage 2 below."

1½ mugs **basmati rice**

1 mug defrosted **frozen peas**

Sauce

1 **fat red chilli**, deseeded (optional)

3 cloves **garlic**

2 tablespoons freshly-grated **ginger**

30g fresh **coriander**

1 **onion**, cut into chunks

1 teaspoon **black mustard seeds**

1 teaspoon **curry powder**

1 teaspoon **cinnamon**

1 teaspoon **turmeric**

3 **tomatoes**

400ml tin **coconut milk**

1 tablespoon **raw honey**

2 pieces **salmon steak**, cut into bite-sized pieces

250g **cooked prawns**

1   Put the rice in a saucepan with 3 mugs of boiling water. Simmer for 9 minutes. Add the peas to the top of the rice and leave with the lid on until needed.

2   To make the sauce, put everything in a food processor and blitz, or blitz with a hand-held blender. Put in a wok and bring to the boil. Simmer for 5 minutes.

3   Add the fish and simmer gently for 2 minutes.

4   Serve with the rice and peas.

Thai Chicken Stir-Fry

1½ mugs **basmati rice**

2 tablespoons **toasted sesame oil**

3 **chicken breasts**, cut into strips

1 bunch **spring onions**, sliced

2 tablespoons freshly-grated **ginger**

200g **shiitake mushrooms**

2 **pak choi**, sliced

100g **sugar snaps**, halved

Sauce

½ mug **water**

1 **GF chicken stock cube**

1 tablespoon **cornflour**

1 **fat red chilli**, sliced

2 tablespoons **GF soy sauce**

2 tablespoons **raw honey**

1 Add the rice to a saucepan with 3 mugs of boiling water. Bring to the boil and turn down to simmer, with a lid on the pan, for 10 minutes.

2 Meanwhile, heat the oil in a wok and add the chicken. Fry until it is cooked through.

3 Add the spring onions, ginger and mushrooms and fry for 30 seconds.

4 Add the pak choi and sugar snaps and fry for 30 seconds.

5 Mix together the sauce ingredients and add to the wok.

6 Bring to the boil and then serve with the rice.

Why *raw* honey?
See page 9 to understand our approach to sugar

Prawn Pasta with Anchovy Crumb Topping

TIM SAYS: "This anchovy crumb topping is so, so good. The great news is that there is actually plenty more than we have photographed here."

2 slices **GF bread**

8 **anchovies**

1 tablespoon **oil from the anchovy jar**

3 mugs **GF pasta**

1 tablespoon **olive oil**

1 bunch **spring onions**, chopped

500g **cooked prawns**

250g **Philadelphia cheese**

2 tablespoons freshly-chopped **basil**

1 Put the bread, anchovies and oil in a blender, or food processor, and blitz until you have 'breadcrumbs'.

2 Add the pasta to plenty of boiling, salted water and simmer until the pasta is tender. Drain, rinse and return to the pan.

3 Heat a frying pan and add the contents of the processor. Fry on a fairly high heat, stirring frequently until the breadcrumbs are browned and crisp. Set to one side. Wipe the pan with a paper towel.

4 Heat the oil in the frying pan, add the onions and fry for 30 seconds. Add the prawns and heat through.

5 Add the Philadelphia and mix until the cheese melts. Add the basil and stir in. Take off the heat.

6 Drain the pasta and add to the prawn mixture.

7 Serve with the breadcrumbs sprinkled on top.

'Doughless' Pizza

Making gluten-free pizza dough is totally possible (we have a recipe in "NOSH Gluten-Free Baking), but it can be a bit tricky for an everyday recipe. This 'doughless' recipe is a bit of a cheat, but who cares, when you want pizza, you want pizza!

Base

1 mug/110g **garam flour** (chickpea flour)

salt and **pepper**

½ teaspoon **GF baking powder**

1 tablespoon **olive oil**

½ mug/150ml cold **water**

1 tablespoon freshly-chopped **basil**

Topping

110g **prosciutto**

150g **mozzarella cheese**

100g **cherry tomatoes**

3 tablespoons **sundried tomato purée**

1 bunch **spring onions**, chopped

1 bag **green salad**

1 Preheat the grill.

2 Put the base ingredients in a bowl and mix together until smooth.

3 Heat 1 tablespoon of olive oil in a large frying pan. Add the base mixture and cook on a medium heat until the bottom is lightly browned.

4 Place under the grill until the top is browned.

5 Put the tomatoes, tomato purée and spring onions in a processor, or liquidiser, and blend until chunky. Spread over the cooked base.

6 Place the prosciutto and mozzarella on top.

7 Put under the grill for 5–10 minutes until the cheese begins to brown slightly.

8 Tip out of the pan and serve with salad.

Cacciatore Spaghetti

Cacciatore means "hunter" in Italian. So essentially this means a meal prepared "hunter-style". Usually it is made with onions, herbs, tomatoes, peppers and wine. No wine in our recipe, so why not just crack open a bottle.

300g **quinoa spaghetti**

2 tablespoons **olive oil**

150g **smoked bacon**

3 **chicken breasts**, cut into bite-sized pieces

250 **chestnut mushrooms**, chopped

Sauce

1 **red onion**, cut into 4

1 **red pepper**, deseeded and cut into 4

6 **tomatoes**, halved

1 clove **garlic**, whole

2 tablespoons freshly-chopped **basil**

1 tablespoon **cornflour**

1 **GF chicken stock cube**

2 tablespoons **tomato purée**

1 Put the spaghetti in a large pan of boiling, salted water and simmer for 9 minutes. Drain, rinse under hot water and return to the pan.

2 Meanwhile, heat the oil in a wok or large frying pan. Add the bacon and fry until crisp. Take out of the pan and chop into bite-sized pieces.

3 Add the chicken and fry until it is no longer pink on the outside. Add the mushrooms and fry for 1 minute.

4 Put the sauce ingredients in a liquidiser or food processor. Whizz until smooth.

5 Add to the pan with the chicken mixture, along with the bacon. Bring to the boil and simmer for 3–4 minutes.

6 Serve with the spaghetti.

Sausage Ragu

A typical, good, hearty ragu packed with flavour. Lovely sweetness from the apples, with 'umptuous' nuggets of caramelised sausage.

Sauce

6 **tomatoes**

1 **red onion**, peeled and cut into large wedges

1 tablespoon **cornflour**

1 **GF veg stock cube**

1 clove **garlic**, peeled

1 tablespoon **GF balsamic vinegar**

2 tablespoons **sun-dried tomato purée**

2½ mugs **GF pasta**

1 tablespoon **olive oil**

600g **GF sausages**, de-skinned

2 **Pink Lady apples**, cut into small chunks.

1 tablespoon freshly-chopped **basil**, to serve

1 Put the sauce ingredients in a food processor or liquidiser and blitz until smooth. Set to one side until needed.

2 Add the pasta to plenty of boiling, salted water and simmer until the pasta is tender. Drain, rinse and return to the pan.

3 Meanwhile, heat the oil in a large frying pan. Pinch up each of the sausages and add to the frying pan. Fry until browned. Keep stirring the sausages and breaking them up as you go.

4 Once the sausages are browned, add the sauce, season well with salt and pepper and cook for 3–4 minutes. Stir occasionally.

5 Add the apple and cook for 1 minute.

6 Add the contents of the frying pan to the pasta pan and mix.

7 Serve with the basil sprinkled over the top.

VEGE-TARIAN

when meat just isn't your bag

Parsnip and Potato Rosti with Halloumi and Pomegranate

Savoury rosti with pops of sweetness from cherry tomatoes and pomegranate seeds. Topped off with fried cheese and caramelised onions. Who wouldn't like that?

2 medium **potatoes**

2 medium **parsnips**

2 tablespoons **olive oil**

1 **onion**, chopped

200g **cherry tomatoes**

100g **pomegranate seeds**

1 tablespoon **raw honey**

1 tablespoon **cider vinegar**

250g **halloumi**, sliced

1 Grate the potatoes and parsnips, or put in the processor with the grater blade. Mix together and season with salt and pepper.

2 Heat the oil in a large frying pan, put 4 piles of the mixture in and squash down. Fry gently, turn over and fry the other side. Fry in batches if necessary and keep warm in a low oven.

3 Fry the onion until browned and softened. Add the tomatoes and fry for 2 minutes. Add the pomegranate seeds, honey and vinegar and cook for 1 minute.

4 Heat a little oil in a frying pan and fry the halloumi until browned on both sides. Serve.

Why *raw* honey?

See page 9 to understand our approach to sugar

Kitcherie

TIM SAYS: "If you are ever looking for a way to kill time, try researching the difference between a Kitcherie and a Kedgerie. You end up with a sore head and no answers!? All I can say is they are pretty much the same thing and I am sure life it too short to try to find a definitive answer."

2 tablespoons **olive oil**

1 **onion**, chopped

1 clove **garlic**, chopped

1/2 **fat red chilli**, chopped

1 teaspoon freshly-grated **ginger**

3/4 mug **basmati rice**

1 teaspoon **turmeric**

1 teaspoon **coriander**

1 teaspoon **cumin**

11/2 mugs **water**

6–8 **eggs**

1 mug defrosted **frozen peas**

100g **spinach**, roughly chopped

1 Heat the oil in a large frying pan and fry the onion until it begins to soften. Add the garlic, chilli, ginger, rice, turmeric, coriander and cumin. Fry for 30 seconds.

2 Add the water and bring to the boil. Simmer, with a lid on the pan for 10 minutes.

3 Put the eggs in a separate pan of boiling water and simmer for 5 minutes. Drain the eggs, run under a cold tap and carefully peel.

4 Add the peas and spinach to the rice mix and heat through.

5 Serve with the soft-boiled eggs.

Why use a *mug*?

See page 7 to see why we love mugs so much

£2.08 /PERSON | SERVES 4 | EASE ★★☆☆☆ | PREP 20 MINS | V

Tahini Noodles with Chunky Mimosa

TIM SAYS: "As 'everyone' knows a mimosa is a tree with a delicate, fine, yellow blossom. We have gone with a chunky mimosa here, because Ben and I thought it looked better! You can chop the egg up a little finer and see which you prefer."

150g **ribbon rice noodles**

6 **eggs**

200g **green beans**, halved

200g **baby sweetcorn**, cut into strips

200g **mangetout**, cut into thin slices

Sauce

3 tablespoons **tahini**

3 tablespoons **toasted sesame oil**

juice of a **lemon**

1½ tablespoons **raw honey**

1½ tablespoons **GF soy sauce**

1 Put the rice noodles in a large bowl, cover with boiling water and leave to soak for about 8–10 minutes. Drain.

2 Put the eggs in a pan of boiling water and simmer gently for 10 minutes. Drain and rinse in cold water.

3 Put the green beans in a pan of boiling water and simmer for 3 minutes.

4 Add the sweetcorn and mangetout to the pan and simmer for a further 1 minute.

5 Drain and mix with the rice noodles.

6 To make the sauce, mix the ingredients together thoroughly.

7 Peel the eggs and chop.

8 Serve the noodle mixture on to the plates. Add the eggs on top and drizzle with the sauce.

Vegetable Risotto with Goat's Cheese

A quick one-pot dish which contrasts the fresh, crunchy vegetables and the warm, 'gooey', grilled goat's cheese.

2 tablespoons **toasted sesame oil**

3 **carrots**, peeled and diced

3 sticks **celery**, sliced

1 **red onion**, sliced

³/₄ mug **basmati rice**

1½ mugs **water**

1 **GF veg stock cube**

1 mug defrosted **frozen soy beans**

zest of a **lemon**

200g **sugar snaps**, sliced in half

2 tablespoons freshly-chopped **basil**

200g **goat's cheese**, cut into 1cm thick rings

1 Heat the oil in a large frying pan. Add the carrots, celery and onion and fry until the onion begins to brown.

2 Add the rice and cook for 1 minute. Add the water and stock and bring to the boil. Turn down to simmer, with a lid on the pan, for 5 minutes.

3 Preheat the grill.

4 Add the soybeans and simmer, with the lid on the pan, for a further 5 minutes.

5 Add the lemon zest, sugar snaps and basil and mix together.

6 Arrange the goat's cheese over the top and then put under the grill until the cheese browns.

Nut Roast with Squash and Avocado Salad

1 **butternut squash**

1 teaspoon **paprika**

1 teaspoon **dried rosemary**

2 tablespoons **olive oil**

25g **butter**

1 **onion**, sliced

2 cloves **garlic**, finely chopped

200g **Brazil nuts**

100g **hazelnuts**

150g **mushrooms**

250g **chestnuts**

4 **eggs**

1 mug grated **Cheddar cheese**

20 **black olives**, roughly chopped

2 **avocados**, cut into chunks

1 bag **rocket salad**

Dressing

1 tablespoon **raw honey**

juice of a **lemon**

1 tablespoon **tahini**

2 tablespoons **extra virgin olive oil**

salt and **pepper**

1 Preheat the oven to 180°C fan oven/200°C/gas 6.

2 Peel the butternut squash and cut into bite-sized chunks. Place on a roasting tray with the paprika, rosemary and oil. Mix together and place in the oven for 40 minutes.

3 To make the nut roast, heat the butter in a small pan and fry the onion and garlic until browned.

4 Put the Brazil nuts and hazelnuts in a food processor and whizz, but leave them a bit chunky. Add the mushrooms and chestnuts and pulse a few times. Add the eggs and cheese, season with salt and pepper and pulse a few times. Turn into a greased dish and bake in the oven for 25 minutes.

5 Once the squash is cooked and lightly browned, take out of the oven and mix with the olives and avocados. Serve on top of the rocket salad, with the combined dressing ingredients on top.

Mushroom and Cashew Pasta

Perfect for those days when you want something quick and simple and... meatless.

3 mugs **GF pasta**

25g **butter**

1 bunch **spring onions**, sliced

250g **chestnut mushrooms**, sliced

1 mug **cashews**

150g **Philadelphia cheese**

1/2 mug **water**

1 **GF veg stock cube**

1 **fat red chilli**, sliced

2 tablespoons freshly-chopped **basil**

Parmesan to serve on top

1 Add the pasta to plenty of boiling, salted water and simmer until the pasta is tender. Drain, rinse and return to the pan.

2 Meanwhile, heat the butter in a large frying pan, or wok, add the onions and fry for 30 seconds.

3 Add the mushrooms and fry for 1 minute. Season well with salt and pepper.

4 Add the cashews, Philadelphia, water and stock cube and bring to the boil.

5 Simmer for 2 minutes, stirring to ensure the Philadelphia melts.

6 Add the cooked pasta, chilli and basil and mix.

7 Serve with the Parmesan on top.

£ 2.41 /PERSON — SERVES 4 — EASE ★★★☆☆ — PREP 15 MINS — COOK 40 MINS — V

Roast Chickpea and Tomato Salad with Fried Halloumi

We have used smoked paprika here. It is in 'another world' compared with regular paprika. Whereas regular paprika is crushed dried chillies, smoked paprika uses chillies which are smoke-dried and then crushed. They are often smoked with oak which gives a strong earthy flavour.

2 **red onions**, cut into wedges

3 **sweet potatoes**, unpeeled and cut into small chunks

400g tin **chickpeas**, rinsed and drained

300g **cherry tomatoes**

1 tablespoon **smoked paprika**

4 tablespoons **olive oil**

1 tablespoon **olive oil**

2 x 250g blocks **halloumi**, cut into slices

1 tablespoon freshly-chopped **coriander**

2 **Cos lettuces**, thinly sliced

Dressing

1 tablespoon **extra virgin olive oil**

juice of a **lemon**

1 teaspoon **Dijon mustard**

1 tablespoon **raw honey**

1 Preheat the oven to 180°C fan oven/200°C/gas 6.

2 Put the onion, sweet potatoes, chickpeas and tomatoes on a large roasting tray. Sprinkle the paprika over and season with salt and pepper. Then drizzle the oil over. Mix everything together with your hands. Place in the oven for 40 minutes.

3 When the roast veggies are cooked, heat the next tablespoon of oil in a large frying pan. Add the halloumi and cook on quite a high heat until browned on each side.

4 Add the coriander to the roast veg and gently stir.

5 Serve with the lettuce and the combined dressing ingredients.

Brazil Nut Burgers

4 **potatoes**, cut into wedges

2 tablespoons **olive oil**

75g **Brazil nuts**

1 **onion**, quartered

2 cloves **garlic**, peeled

½ teaspoon **smoked paprika**

salt and **pepper**

2 medium slices **GF bread**

200g **chestnut mushrooms**

2 tablespoons freshly-chopped **coriander**

1 **egg yolk**

Salad

1 **Little Gem lettuce**, sliced

1 **fat red chilli**, chopped

½ **cucumber**, cut into small cubes

2 **carrots**, grated

Dressing

2 tablespoons **Greek yoghurt**

1 tablespoon **raw honey**

juice of a **lime**

2 tablespoons **olive oil**

salt and **pepper**

1 Preheat the oven to 200°C fan oven/180°C/gas 6. Put the potato wedges on a tray, cover with the oil and bake for 40 minutes.

2 Put the Brazil nuts, onion, garlic, paprika, salt and pepper and bread in a food processor and whizz, but not too fine. Add the mushrooms and pulse a few times. Add the coriander and egg yolk and pulse a few times.

3 Turn out onto a board and squash together. Form into 4 burgers. Put in the fridge until needed.

4 Mix together the salad ingredients in a large bowl. Mix together the dressing ingredients and add to the salad.

5 Heat a tablespoon of oil in a frying pan and fry the burgers on a medium heat for 3 minutes each side. They should be nicely browned.

6 Serve with the potato wedges and salad.

Baked Potatoes with Roast Veg and Feta

4 **potatoes**

1 **red onion**, cut into wedges

1 **courgette**, sliced

2 **sweet potatoes**, cut into 2cm chunks

4 **tomatoes**, cut into wedges

2 tablespoons **olive oil**

1 teaspoon **cumin**

1 teaspoon **coriander**

Feta sauce

200g **feta cheese**

1 tablespoon **lemon juice**

salt and **pepper**

200ml **soured cream**

2 tablespoons freshly-chopped **coriander**

1 Preheat the oven to 180°C fan oven/200°C/gas 6. Make a cut in the top of each potato and rub with a little oil. Season with salt and place on a baking tray. Bake in the oven for 1 hour.

2 Meanwhile, put the rest of the vegetables on a roasting tray. Drizzle with the oil, sprinkle over the spices, season with salt and pepper and spread out on the tray. Roast in the oven for 50 minutes.

3 Meanwhile, put the sauce ingredients in a processor, or liquidizer, and whizz to make a cream.

4 Break open the potatoes and put the roasted veg on top. Serve with the feta sauce.

Gardener's Pie

So, we might well have made up the term 'garden pie' in pursuit of an appropriate name for a vegetarian Shepherd's Pie. We'll find out if it catches on. Make sure you buy the pre-cooked chestnuts in the vacuum pack for this one. It will definitely not work with the hard ones in the little, net bags.

4 medium **potatoes**, no need to peel, cut into 2cm cubes

20g **butter**

1 tablespoon **olive oil**

1 **red onion**, chopped

1 tablespoon **dried rosemary**

1 **courgette**, chopped

200g **cooked chestnuts**, chopped

300g **chestnut mushrooms**, chopped

1 tablespoon **GF flour**

2 tablespoons **sun-dried tomato purée**

1 mug **water**

1 **GF veg stock cube**

1 mug grated **Cheddar cheese**

1 Preheat the oven to 180°C fan oven/200°C/gas 6.

2 Put the potatoes in a pan of boiling water. Simmer for 10 minutes, drain and add the butter. Set to one side until needed.

3 Heat the oil in a wok or large frying pan. Fry the onions until they are browned.

4 Add the rosemary and courgette and fry for 2 minutes.

5 Add the chestnuts and the mushrooms and fry for 2 minutes. Add the flour and mix.

6 Add the tomato purée, water and stock. Season well and bring to the boil. Pour into a casserole dish.

7 Spread the potatoes over the top and sprinkle over the cheese.

8 Bake in the oven for 25 minutes or until the cheese browns a little.

Vegetable Risotto with 'Angry' Eggs

Sometimes you might find that your chillies don't give you the heat you are looking for. One trick is to cook them for a little longer, as that gives the capsicum (the hot stuff) time to infuse into the rest of dish.

25g **butter**

1 bunch **spring onions**

2 **carrots**, peeled and cut into small cubes

3 sticks **celery**, chopped

1 **red pepper**, chopped

1 mug **basmati rice**

1/2 **fat red chilli**, deseeded and chopped

1 **GF veg stock cube**

4 **eggs**

1   Heat the butter in a large frying pan.

2   Add the onions, carrots, celery and peppers and fry for 1 minute.

3   Add the rice and half the chilli and fry for 1 minute.

4   Season well with salt and pepper and add 2 mugs of boiling water, plus the stock cube. Put a lid, or cover, on the pan and simmer for 10 minutes.

5   Fry the eggs and sprinkle with the rest of the chilli as they cook. Serve with the rice.

Why use a *mug*?

See page 7 to see why we love mugs so much

TAKE YOUR TIME

for those rare times when you
have time to kill

Crackled Pork with Creamed Spinach and Roasties

1kg **belly pork**, cut into 4 pieces

5 medium **potatoes**, cut into 2cm chunks

25g **butter**

1 **onion**, chopped

1 clove **garlic**, sliced

1 tablespoon **GF flour**

1¼ mugs **milk**

150g **Philadelphia cheese**

¼ teaspoon **nutmeg**

250g **spinach**, chopped

¾ mug grated **Parmesan**

1 Put the belly pork on a rack in a roasting tray. Season well with salt and pepper. Pour 3 mugs of water into the tray, cover with foil and roast in the oven for 1 hour.

2 After 1 hour take the foil off and return to the oven for a further 2 hours. If the skin is not crisp at the end, whack under the grill for a couple of minutes.

3 Place the potatoes on a roasting tray. Drizzle with olive oil and season well with salt and pepper. Mix everything together with your hands. Roast in the oven for 50 minutes.

4 When the meat has 30 minutes left to cook, make the creamed spinach. First, preheat the grill. Heat the butter in a large pan or wok, add the onions and garlic and fry until the onion begins to soften. Season well with salt and pepper.

5 Add the flour and mix well. Add the milk and bring to the boil. The sauce should thicken.

6 Add the Philadelphia and nutmeg and simmer gently to allow the cheese to melt.

7 Add the chopped spinach and cook until it begins to wilt. Pour the mixture into an ovenproof casserole dish. Spread the Parmesan over the top.

8 Place under the grill until the cheese browns and bubbles.

9 Serve with the pork and potatoes.

Chicken Tagine with Cauliflower 'Couscous'

BEN SAYS: "As I am sure you could have guessed, growing up, I was not a big fan of cauliflower. I think if mum had tried cooking it like this, there might have been a chance I would have liked it. I certainly really like this one."

2 tablespoons **olive oil**

2 **onions**, sliced

750g **boneless, skinless chicken thighs**, sliced

1 tablespoon **GF flour**

3 cloves **garlic**, finely chopped

1 tablespoon freshly-grated **ginger**

1 teaspoon **turmeric**

2 mugs **water**

1 **GF chicken stock cube**

juice of a **lemon**

1 mug **ready-to-eat dried apricots**, roughly chopped

1 **cauliflower**

2 tablespoons **olive oil**

juice of ½ **lemon**

3 tablespoons freshly-chopped **coriander**

¼ mug **flaked almonds**

1 Preheat the oven to 180°C fan oven/200°C/gas 6.

2 Heat the oil in a large hob-to-oven casserole dish. Add the onions and fry until they begin to soften.

3 Add the chicken and fry until it is no longer pink.

4 Add the flour and mix well.

5 Add the garlic, ginger, turmeric, water, stock, lemon and apricots and mix together. Bring to the boil and simmer until the sauce thickens slightly.

6 Cook in the oven for 45 minutes.

7 Meanwhile, make the 'couscous'. Cut the leaves and thick stalk from the cauliflower and break into florets. Place in the processor and blitz until you have something resembling breadcrumbs, but don't make it too fine.

8 10 minutes before the end of the cooking-time for the chicken, heat the oil in a large frying pan and add the cauliflower. Cook gently on a medium heat, stirring frequently for 5 minutes. Add the lemon juice and coriander and mix.

9 Serve with the chicken.

10 Sprinkle the flaked almonds over the top when you serve.

Chicken Poutine

This is classic Canadian, comfort food. Traditionally it is served with French fries, so here is a great opportunity for our oven-cooked potato wedges.

4 large **potatoes**, cut into wedges

2 tablespoons **olive oil**

Sauce

1 **onion**, sliced

50g **butter**

1 tablespoon **GF flour**

2 tablespoons **sun-dried tomato purée**

1 mug **water**

1 **GF veg stock cube**

1 tablespoon **olive oil**

3 **chicken breasts**, cut into bite-sized pieces

2 **mozzarella balls**

2 tablespoons freshly-chopped **basil**

1 Preheat the oven to 180°C fan oven/200C/gas 6. Put the wedges in a large casserole dish, drizzle over the oil, season with salt and pepper and mix everything together. Place in the oven for 45 minutes, or until the wedges are nice and brown.

2 Meanwhile, make the sauce. Put the onion and butter in a medium-sized saucepan and fry until the onion begins to soften. Add the flour and stir.

3 Add the rest of the sauce ingredients and bring to the boil, stirring frequently. Set to one side until needed. Preheat the grill.

4 Heat the oil in a large frying pan and fry the chicken until it is just cooked through.

5 Take the wedges out of the oven and spread the chicken over them.

6 Tear up the mozzarella and spread over the chicken.

7 Put under a hot grill until the mozzarella begins to bubble and brown a little.

8 Reheat the sauce and pour over the top. Sprinkle the over basil.

Mustard Chicken with Sweet Potato Roasties and Lemon Dill Coleslaw

2 tablespoons **virgin coconut oil**

2–3 **sweet potatoes**, peeled and cut into 2cm chunks.

3 **chicken breasts**

1 **egg**, beaten

3 tablespoons **cornflour**

1 tablespoon **dried mustard**

1 tablespoon **olive oil**

2 tablespoons **raw honey**

Coleslaw

juice of ½ **lemon**

2 tablespoons freshly-chopped **dill**

2 tablespoons freshly-chopped **mint**

3 tablespoons **mayo**

1 medium **carrot**, grated

1 **hearts of romaine lettuce**, thinly sliced

4 **spring onions**, sliced lengthways

½ mug **raisins**

1   Preheat the oven to 180°C fan oven/200°C/gas 6. Put 2 tablespoons of coconut oil on a roasting tray and place in the oven for 2–3 minutes to melt.

2   Add the sweet potatoes, mix everything together, season with salt and pepper and roast in the oven for 40 minutes.

3   Put the chicken breast between some cling film and give it a bash with a rolling pin until it is about 1cm thick. Dip the chicken in the beaten egg.

4   Mix together the cornflour, mustard and salt and pepper on a large plate. Press the chicken into the mixture and attach as much as possible.

5   Heat the oil in a large frying pan and fry the chicken on a fairly high heat for about 2–3 minutes each side. Check that it is cooked through. Drizzle over the honey. Remove from the pan and cut into long slices.

6   Mix together the coleslaw ingredients and serve with the chicken and the roasties.

Why virgin coconut oil?
Not only can it taste great, but it has amazing health benefits too.

£ 1.31 /PERSON SERVES 4 EASE ★★☆☆☆ PREP 20 MINS COOK 30 MINS

Lyonnaise Potatoes with Roasted Sausage

A good hearty dish, fashioned in a French style.

2 **onions**, sliced

1 tablespoon **olive oil**

50g **butter**

4 **potatoes**, thickly sliced

8 **GF sausages**

1 **GF beef stock cube**

1 mug boiling **water**

savoy cabbage

25g **butter**

1   Preheat the oven to 180°C fan oven/200°c/gas 6.

2   Put the onions, oil, butter and potatoes in a hob-to-oven casserole dish. Take the skins off the sausages and 'pinch' into pieces and add to the dish. Fry until some of the contents begin to brown. Stir frequently.

3   Add the stock and water and bring to the boil. Simmer for 5 minutes to get everything heated through. Season well with salt and pepper. Roast in the oven for 30 minutes.

4   5 minutes before the end of the cooking-time, put the cabbage in a pan and add about a mug of boiling water. Simmer for 4 minutes. Drain and return to the pan. Add the 25g butter and season well with pepper. Cook for 1 minute in the butter.

5   Serve with the potatoes.

Super Mash with Pan Roasted Chicken, Cavolo Nero and Balsamic Sauce

4 **carrots**, cut into dice

1/2 **celeriac**, cut into 2cm chunks

2 **sweet potatoes**, peeled and cut into 2cm chunks

2 tablespoons **Philadelphia cheese**

2 tablespoons freshly-chopped **chives**

1 tablespoon **olive oil**

3 **chicken breasts**

200g **cavolo nero**

1 **red onion**, sliced

Sauce

1 mug **water**

1 **GF chicken stock cube**

1 tablespoon **cornflour**

1 tablespoon **Gf soy sauce**

1 tablespoon **GF balsamic vinegar**

1 tablespoon **pure maple syrup**

1   Put the carrots in a large saucepan with plenty of boiling water. Bring to the boil and then simmer for 5 minutes. Add the celeriac and simmer for a further 5 minutes.

2   Add the sweet potato and simmer for another 5 minutes. Drain and return to the pan with the Philadelphia and chives. Mash together. Replace the lid on the pan and set to one side until needed.

3   Meanwhile, heat the oil in a frying pan and fry the chicken breast for 2 minutes each side on a high heat. Season well with salt and pepper. Turn down the heat and fry on a low heat for a further 4 minutes each side.

4   Put the cavolo nero in a pan of boiling water. Simmer for 6 minutes. Drain and return to the pan.

5   Add the onions to the frying pan. Fry until they begin to soften. Mix the sauce ingredients together, add to the pan and bring to the boil. Simmer for 1 minute.

6   Slice the chicken and share amongst the plates. Serve with the mash, cavolo nero and sauce.

Why *pure* maple syrup?

Lamb Shoulder with Coconut Roasties and Kale

1.5kg **lamb shoulder**

1 teaspoon **cumin**

1 teaspoon **coriander**

2 mugs **water**

3 tablespoons **virgin coconut oil**

5 **potatoes**, cut into 2cm chunks

200g **kale**

1 mug defrosted **frozen peas**

25g softened **butter**

2 tablespoons **GF flour**

2 tablespoons freshly-chopped **mint**

1 Preheat the oven to 180°C fan oven/200°C/gas 6. Put the shoulder of lamb in a large casserole dish. Sprinkle over the cumin and coriander and season well with salt and pepper, Rub the mixture into the skin. Put the 2 mugs of water in the bottom of the dish. Cover and place in the oven for 1 hour.

2 After an hour, turn down the oven to 150°C fan oven/170°C/gas 4 and cook for a further 4 hours. Leave to rest. Cover with two towels to keep warm.

3 Turn the oven up to 200°C fan oven/220°C/gas 7. Put the coconut oil in a large roasting tray and place in the oven for 5 minutes.

4 Take the roasting tray out of the oven and add the potatoes, carefully turning the potatoes over to mix in the oil. Season with salt and pepper. Roast in the oven for 50 minutes, or until browned.

5 Near the end of the cooking-time, put the kale on to simmer for 4 minutes. Add the peas and simmer for 1 minute. Drain and return to the pan.

6 Meanwhile, make the gravy. Take the meat out of the casserole dish. Skim off the fat from the top of the juices and discard. Mix together the butter and flour and add the mint. Add to the meat juices and mix well.. Bring to the boil and simmer for 1 minute.

7 Serve the meat with the roasties, kale and gravy.

Swedish Meatballs with Blackberry Sauce

Meatballs

1 **onion**, quartered

1 slice **GF bread**

350g **minced beef**

350g **minced pork**

½ teaspoon **allspice**

zest of a **lemon**

½ teaspoon **nutmeg**

2 **egg** yolks

5 medium **potatoes**, cut into 2cm chunks

25g **butter**

25g **butter**

2 tablespoons **GF flour**

1 mug **water** +
GF beef stock cube

200ml **soured cream**

2 tablespoons freshly-chopped **parsley**

200g **blackberries**

1 tablespoon **pure maple syrup**

1 Preheat the oven to 180°C fan oven/200°C/fas 6. Grease a roasting tray.

2 To make the meatballs, put the meatball ingredients in a food processor, season with salt and pepper and pulse together (if you don't have a processor, just chop everything finely and mix together).

3 Form into 20 meatballs. Put them on the roasting tray and bake in the oven for 25 minutes.

4 Put the potatoes in a pan of boiling water. Simmer for 10 minutes. Drain and mash together with the butter. Put the lid back on the pan until needed.

5 To make the gravy, put the butter and flour in a small saucepan over a medium heat and mix together. Add the water and stock and bring to the boil, stirring frequently. The sauce should thicken. Add the soured cream and parsley and season well with salt and pepper.

6 To make the blackberry sauce, just put the blackberries in a small pan and heat. Add the maple syrup and allow to simmer for 2–3 minutes. Squash with a fork.

7 Serve the meatballs with the mash, gravy and blackberry sauce.

Why *pure* maple syrup?
See page 9 to understand our approach to sugar

Turkish Lamb and Hummus on Sourdough Toast

Hummus

juice of a **lemon**

3 tablespoons **olive oil**

400g tin **chickpeas**, rinsed and drained

3 tablespoons **tahini**

salt and **pepper**

2 tablespoons **olive oil**

1 **onion**, sliced

2 cloves **garlic**, finely chopped

500g **lamb mince**

1 teaspoon **cumin seeds**

1 teaspoon **smoked paprika**

2 tablespoons **tomato purée**

²/₃ mug/200ml **water**

¹/₂ mug **pecans**, chopped

4 slices **GF sourdough bread**, lightly toasted

150ml **soured cream**

1 bag **green salad**,

1　To make the hummus, put all the ingredients in a food processor, or blender, and blitz until smooth.

2　Heat the oil in a large frying pan and add the onions and garlic. Fry until the onions soften.

3　Add the mince and fry until no longer pink.

4　Add the rest of the ingredients and simmer for 10 minutes.

5　Serve by spreading the hummus on the toasted bread. Add the lamb mixture on top, along with a good dollop of the soured cream.

6　Serve with salad.

Indonesian Roast Chicken

TIM SAYS: "This is one of my absolute favourites from this book. The day we first tested it, I loved it so much, that I made it again the very same day for people we had around for a meal."

2 **onions**, cut into wedges

4 cloves **garlic**, peeled and left whole

1 **fat red chilli**, sliced

1.5kg **whole chicken**

3 tablespoons **GF soy sauce**

zest and juice of a **lime**

2 tablespoons freshly-grated **ginger**

2 tablespoons **raw honey**

1 tablespoon **shrimp paste**

400ml tin **coconut milk**

1 mug **basmati rice**

1 fresh, ripe **mango**

juice of a **lime**

2 tablespoons freshly-chopped **coriander**

1 Preheat the oven to 180°C fan oven/200°C/gas 6.

2 Place the onion wedges, garlic, chilli and the chicken in a roasting tray.

3 Mix together the soy, lime, ginger, honey, shrimp paste and coconut milk. Pour over the chicken and mix everything together with your hands, making sure that the chicken is well covered.

4 Put foil over the chicken and roast in the oven.

5 After 30 minutes remove the foil, baste the chicken in the juices and return to the oven.

6 After another 30 minutes, baste once more and return to the oven for the final 30 minutes. The chicken should then be browned and the sauce thickened.

7 Add the rice to a saucepan with 2 mugs of boiling water. Bring to the boil and then turn down to simmer, with a lid on the pan, for 10 minutes.

8 Stir in the mango and coriander and serve with the chicken and sauce from the roasting tray.

Why *raw* honey?

See page 9 to understand our approach to sugar

Slow-Cooked Hot and Sour Beef Noodles

We often think of noodle dishes as fast meals with quickly fried meats and vegetables, but they don't have to be. They can have slow-cooked meat with all the flavours that only come with time. Really worth waiting for this one.

1 tablespoon **olive oil**

750g **beef stewing steak**

2 cloves **garlic**, chopped

4 **anchovies**, chopped

1 tablespoon **GF flour**

2 mugs **water**

1 **GF beef stock cube**

200g **rice noodles**

2 **pak choi**, chopped

1 **fat red chilli**, chopped

1 bunch **spring onions**, chopped

2 tablespoons **GF fish sauce**

2 tablespoons **pure maple syrup**

3 tablespoons freshly-chopped **coriander**

1   Preheat the oven to 180°C fan oven/200°C/gas 6.

2   Heat the oil in a large hob-to-oven casserole. Add the beef, garlic and anchovies and fry until the meat is no longer pink on the outside.

3   Season well with salt and pepper. Add the flour and stir well. Add the water and stock cube. Bring to the boil.

4   Put a lid on the casserole and cook in the oven for 1½ hours.

5   Put the rice noodles in a large bowl and pour over enough boiling water to cover them. Leave for 5 minutes. Add the pak choi and leave for 2 minutes. Drain and return to the bowl.

6   Take the casserole out of the oven. Add the chilli, spring onions, fish sauce and maple syrup to the meat. Bring to the boil.

7   Add the coriander and stir. Serve with the rice noodles and pak choi.

Why *pure* maple syrup?

See page 9 to understand our approach to sugar

Pork Casserole with Pomme Anna

1kg **new potatoes**

100g **thinly sliced ham**

2 tablespoons **olive oil**

2 tablespoons **olive oil**

2 **onions**, sliced

750g **diced pork shoulder**

2 cloves **garlic**, finely chopped

2 tablespoons **GF flour**

1½ mugs **water**

1 **GF veg stock cube**

2 **carrots**, sliced

2 tablespoons **GF balsamic vinegar**

1 tablespoon **raw honey**

20 **green olives**

2 teaspoons **dried oregano**

200g **kale**

1 Preheat the oven to 180°C fan oven/200°C/gas 6.

2 Grease a 20cm cake tin or flan dish.

3 Slice the potatoes thinly using the slicing blade on your food processor.

4 Put the potatoes and oil in a bowl, season with salt and pepper and mix together. Arrange the potatoes in layers in the cake tin and divide the ham evenly between the layers. Cover the tin with foil and bake in the oven for 1 hour.

5 Meanwhile, make the casserole. Heat the oil in a large frying pan and fry the onions until they begin to soften. Season well with salt and pepper.

6 Add the pork and the garlic and fry until the meat is no longer pink on the outside.

7 Add the flour and mix well.

8 Add the rest of the ingredients, apart from the kale, and bring to the boil. Place in the oven for 1½ hours.

9 After the potatoes have been in the oven for 1 hour, remove the foil. Put back in the oven for another 45 minutes to allow it to brown on top.

10 Put the kale in a pan of boiling, salted water and simmer for 5 minutes. Drain and serve with the potatoes and stew.

Easy Russian Fish Pie

The reason we have called this one 'easy' is because, traditionally, a Russian fish pie would have the pastry around the whole thing, like a huge Cornish pasty. In this one we have just laid it over the top to keep it simple.

4 **eggs**

50g **butter**

1 **onion**, chopped

¹⁄₃ mug **basmati rice**

1 **GF fish stock cube**

250g **chestnut mushrooms**, sliced

300g **white fish**, cut into bite-sized pieces

1 tablespoon freshly-chopped **dill**

150g **cooked prawns**

280g **GF ready-rolled puff pastry**

1 **egg**, beaten

1 Preheat the oven to 200°C fan oven/220°C/gas 7.

2 Put the eggs in a pan of boiling water and simmer for 10 minutes. Drain and rinse with cold water and peel.

3 Heat the butter in a frying pan, add the onion and fry the onion until it begins to soften. Season with salt and pepper. Add the rice, 1 mug of water and the stock cube and simmer, with a lid on the pan, for 10 minutes. Add the mushrooms, fish, dill and prawns to the pan and mix.

4 Pile the fish mixture into a casserole dish. Push the eggs into the mixture. Wet the edges of the dish with water. Put the pastry sheet over the mixture, folding in the pastry so as not to waste any. Brush with the beaten egg.

5 Place in the oven for 30 minutes. The pastry should be nicely browned and crisp.

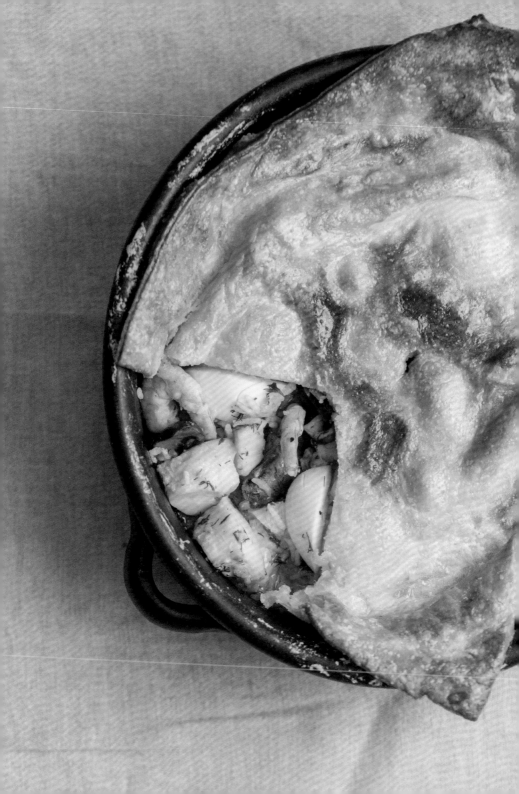

Sweet Quinoa Salad with Roast Chicken Thighs

8 **chicken thighs**, skin on

1 teaspoon **paprika**

2 tablespoons **olive oil**

4 medium **carrots**, peeled and sliced

2 **red onions**, cut into wedges

¹/₂ **red chilli**, chopped

³/₄ mug **quinoa**

¹/₂ mug/75g **raisins**

3 tablespoons **pine nuts**

1 Preheat the oven to 180°C fan oven/200°C/gas 6

2 Put the chicken thighs on a plate and sprinkle with the paprika and oil. Rub into the skins. Place on a roasting tray and roast in the oven for 45 minutes.

3 Put the carrots on a separate dish, drizzle with the oil and season well with salt and pepper. Roast in the oven for 10 minutes. Add the onions and chilli, mix everything together and roast for a further 30 minutes.

4 20 minutes from the end of the cooking-time, put the quinoa in a pan of boiling water and simmer for 20 minutes. Drain.

5 Take the veg out of the oven and stir in the raisins, quinoa and pine nuts.

6 Serve with the chicken thighs on top.

Why use a *mug*?

See page 7 to see why we love mugs so much

Salmon and Dill Pies

4 medium **potatoes** cut into 3cm cubes.

2 tablespoons **olive oil**

250g pack **GF puff pastry**

4 small **salmon steaks**

2 tablespoons **soured cream**

1 tablespoon freshly-chopped **dill**

zest of a **lemon**

1 **egg**, beaten

Sauce

5 tablespoons **soured cream**

1/2 **cucumber**, grated

juice of 1/2 **lemon**

1 tablespoon freshly-chopped **dill**

2 mugs defrosted **frozen peas**

1 Preheat the oven to 180°C fan oven/200°C/gas 6.

2 Put the potatoes on a roasting tray and drizzle over the oil. Season well with salt and pepper. Mix everything together and then spread out on the tray. Roast in the oven for 55 minutes.

3 20 minutes into the cooking-time, turn the oven up to 200°C fan oven/220°C/gas 7.

4 Unroll the pastry and cut into 4 oblongs. Place 1 salmon steak onto each piece of pastry.

5 Mix together the 2 tablespoons soured cream, dill and lemon zest. Spread over the top of each salmon steak.

6 Wet the edges of the pastry and fold each one over to contain the fish. Pinch the edges together to seal the parcel. Place on a baking tray and brush with the beaten egg. Place in the oven for 25 minutes.

7 Meanwhile, mix together the sauce ingredients.

8 5 minutes before the end of the cooking-time, add the peas to a pan of boiling water. Simmer for 2 minutes. Drain and add the butter.

9 Serve with the pies and roasties and sauce.

Honey Roast Gammon with Pesto Dauphinoise

1.5kg piece **unsmoked gammon**

25g fresh **basil**

1/2 mug grated **Parmesan**

1/2 mug **water**

5 **potatoes**, thinly sliced

4 **sundried tomatoes**, chopped

2 tablespoons **oil from the sundried tomatoes**

2 tablespoons **raw honey**

1 head **broccoli**

1 mug defrosted **frozen peas**

25g **butter**

1 Put the gammon in a large bowl and cover with water. Leave overnight to soak.

2 Fill a large saucepan with boiling water and simmer the gammon for 1½ hours.

3 Preheat the oven to 180°C fan oven/200°C/gas 6.

4 Put the basil, Parmesan and water in a liquidiser or processor. Blitz.

5 Mix with the potatoes and the sundried tomatoes. Place in the casserole dish and arrange evenly (see photo). Drizzle the tomato oil over the top. When the meat has 30 minutes left to boil, place the potatoes in the oven for 45–50 minutes until the top is nicely browned.

6 Once the meat is cooked, remove from the pan. Remove the skin. Place on a roasting tray, spread the honey over the top and place in the oven for 20 minutes.

7 Cut the broccoli into florets and add to a pan of boiling water. Simmer for 5 minutes. Add the peas and simmer for 1 minute. Drain and return to the pan. Add the butter and mash together.

8 Serve with the potatoes and gammon.

Why raw *honey?*

See page 9 to understand our approach to sugar

Lamb Pie with Chestnut Pastry

1 tablespoon **olive oil**

1 **onion**, sliced

2 cloves **garlic**, sliced

750g **diced shoulder of lamb**

2 tablespoons **GF flour**

1½ mugs **water**

2 **GF veg stock cubes**

250g **mushrooms**, sliced

4 **carrots**, sliced

2 tablespoons freshly-chopped **mint**

Pastry

250g **GF plain flour**

150g **cold butter**

1 teaspoon **xanthan gum**

180g **whole cooked chestnuts**

1 **egg**, beaten

1 beaten **egg** to brush the top

green beans

1   Preheat the oven to 180°C fan oven/200°C/gas 6.

2   Heat the oil in a large hob-to-oven casserole dish. Add the onions and garlic and fry until the onions begin to soften.

3   Add the lamb and fry until it is no longer pink on the outside.

4   Add the flour and mix well. Add the water, stock, mushrooms, carrots and mint and bring to the boil.

5   Put the lid on the casserole dish and bake in the oven for 1½ hours.

6   Half an hour before the end of the cooking-time, make the pastry. Put the flour, butter, xanthan gum and chestnuts in a food processor and whizz until you have something resembling breadcrumbs.

7   Add the egg and enough water to form a dough and pulse a few times until the pastry holds together. Turn out onto a piece of floured cling film (it will help to lift the pastry) and roll the pastry until is big enough to cover your pie dish.

8   Once the lamb is cooked, pour into the pie dish and place the pastry on top. Trim the pastry and pinch the edges and make a small hole in the centre for the steam to come out. Brush the pastry with beaten egg and bake in the oven for 35–40 minutes.

9   Cook the green beans and serve with the pie.

SWEET

sweet, but still no processed
sugar, so you can go crazy...
though, perhaps not too crazy!!

Sticky Toffee Pudding

Medjool dates are a natural substitute for processed sugar and give us a lovely sweetness, as well as a 'stickiness' which helps to 'hold things together' in some of my recipes. They also provide lots of fibre, which is good for cholesterol, together with plenty of good minerals.

100g **softened butter**

100g **virgin coconut sugar**

2 **eggs**

2 tablespoons **water**

100g **Medjool dates**, chopped

100g **GF self-raising flour**

½ teaspoon **xanthan gum**

2 teaspoons **cacao powder**

Sauce

100g **raw honey**

75g **butter**

5 tablespoons **double cream**

pecans for on top

1 Preheat the oven to 160°C fan oven/180°C/gas 6. Grease 4 ramekin dishes with butter and place on a baking tray.

2 Beat together the butter and sugar (don't worry that it does not totally combine). Add the eggs, one at a time, beating well between each addition.

3 Add the rest of the ingredients (except the sauce) and fold in gently.

4 Spoon into the ramekin dishes and bake in the oven for 25 minutes.

5 Meanwhile, put the sauce ingredients in a small saucepan and bring to the boil.

6 Once cooked, turn out the pudding onto a dish and serve with the sauce and a few pecans.

Why virgin coconut sugar?
See page 9 to understand our approach to sugar

Almond and Raspberry Buns

JOY SAYS: "I can't promise the same will happen for you, but when we made these, the 300g of raspberries divided exactly between our 18 cases. It was incredibly satisfying at the time. Fingers crossed it works out that well for you."

115g **softened butter**

4 tablespoons **virgin coconut oil**

200ml **pure maple syrup**

4 **eggs**

zest of a **lemon**

130g **ground almonds**

150g **GF self-raising flour**

1/4 teaspoon **bicarbonate of soda**

1 teaspoon **xanthan gum**

1/2 teaspoon **GF baking powder**

300g **fresh raspberries**

1 Preheat the oven to 170°C fan oven/190°C/gas 5. Prepare the bun tins with 18 cases.

2 Beat together the butter, coconut oil and maple syrup. Don't worry if it appears not to combine.

3 Add the eggs, one at a time, beating well between each addition.

4 Add the lemon zest and the ground almonds and beat well.

5 Add the flour, bicarbonate of soda, xanthan gum and baking powder. Fold in gently until well mixed.

6 Spoon out into the bun cases and press 3 raspberries into each bun.

7 Bake in the oven for 25 minutes.

Nut Crunch with 'instant' Banana Ice Cream

It's best to freeze the bananas overnight. This is a good way to use bananas that you would otherwise throw away for being over-ripe. Slice them and keep them in the freezer for up to 3 months, ready to use at any time.

50g **butter**

50g **virgin coconut sugar**

50g **nut butter**, see page 211

1 **egg** white

50g **GF plain flour**

1/4 teaspoon **xanthan gum**

50g **GF puffed rice**

4 **frozen, chopped bananas**

100ml **double cream**

2 tablespoons **raw honey**

200g **strawberries**, sliced

1 Preheat the oven to 90°C fan oven/110°C/gas 1/4. Line a 20 x 30cm traybake tin.

2 Beat together the butter and coconut sugar. Add the nut butter and beat.

3 Add the egg white and beat.

4 Stir in the rest of the ingredients.

5 Turn out into the traybake tin and spread the mixture out with a palette knife, so that it fills the tray. It should be about 5mm thick.

6 Bake in the oven for 2 hours. Leave to cool.

7 To make the ice cream, simply put the bananas, cream and honey in a food processor and blitz until smooth. Put in the freezer until you are ready to eat, but not for too long as it will become too hard.

8 Serve with the strawberry and broken-up nut brittle.

Why virgin coconut sugar?

See page 9 to understand our approach to sugar

Chocolate Chip Cookies

JOY SAYS: "I am often goaded by Ben into making these cookies. All he needs to say is "go on mum they only take 22 minutes" and I rise to the call every time!"

125g softened **butter**

210g **virgin coconut sugar**

1 **egg**

1 teaspoon **vanilla extract**

100g x **100% cocoa solids chocolate**, chopped, see page 210

225g **GF self-raising flour**

2 tablespoons **cacao powder**

1 teaspoon **xanthan gum**

1 Preheat the oven to 180°C fan oven/200°C/gas 6. Line 2 large baking sheets.

2 Beat together the butter and sugar.

3 Add the egg and beat well. Add the vanilla and beat.

4 Add the rest of the ingredients and fold in gently.

5 Tip the mixture out of the bowl onto a board and make into a long sausage. Cut into 16 pieces. Roll into balls and then place on the baking sheets, pressing them down with your fingers.

6 Place in the oven for 12 minutes.

Chocolate Fudge Fingers

75g x **100% cocoa solids chocolate**, see page 210

2 tablespoons **cacao powder**

200g **virgin coconut sugar**

100ml **hot water**

175g **softened butter**

2 **eggs**

3 tablespoons **soured cream**

110g **GF self-raising flour**

½ teaspoon **GF baking powder**

½ teaspoon **xanthan gum**

75g **Green and Blacks mint chocolate**, or see page 210

1 Preheat the oven to 160°C fan oven/180°C/gas 4. Line a 20 x 30cm traybake tin.

2 Put the chocolate, cacao powder and sugar in a food processor and blitz until you have something resembling breadcrumbs. If you don't have a processor, just chop the chocolate up as finely as you can and mix in with the cacao and sugar.

3 Add the hot water and whizz.

4 Add the softened butter and whizz.

5 Add the eggs and whizz again.

6 Add the soured cream and pulse a couple of times.

7 Add the flour, baking powder and xanthan gum and pulse 2 or 3 times.

8 Pour the mixture into the prepared tin and spread it out. Bake in the oven for 45 minutes.

9 Once cooled, melt the mint chocolate in a bowl over a pan of simmering water. Put the melted chocolate in a plastic food bag. Snip off the corner and drizzle the chocolate over the top of the cake. Once the chocolate has set, cut into fingers.

Why *100% cocoa solids chocolate?*
See page 202 to understand our reasons

Passion Fruit and Banana Tart

CHOCOLATE SHAVING TIPS: 1. Make sure the chocolate is nice and cold. 2. Take the smooth side of the chocolate and firmly, but carefully, scrape with a sharp knife. 3. Don't try to pick up the shavings with your hands, instead, lift with a knife to avoid them melting.

300g **blanched almonds**

100g **Medjool dates**

75g **butter,** melted

1 tablespoon **cacao powder**

300ml **double cream**

2 **bananas**

1 teaspoon **vanilla extract**

100g **Philadelphia cheese**

70g **cashew nut butter,** see page 211

juice of a **lemon**

1 **banana**

2 **passion fruit**

100% cocoa solids chocolate, see page 210

1 Grease and line a 20cm loose-bottomed cake tin.

2 Put the blanched almonds in a processor and whizz, but not too fine. Add the dates and cacao powder and whizz again. Add the melted butter and pulse a few times to mix.

3 Press into the bottom of the tin. Put in the fridge to cool.

4 Beat the cream until stiff.

5 In a separate bowl, mash the bananas and mix in the vanilla, Philadelphia and nut butter. Don't beat but leave a little lumpy.

6 Stir the lemon juice into the cream, add the mashed banana mix and stir gently. Pour over the nut mix in the cake tin and smooth out evenly. Leave in the fridge for 2 hours, then remove from the cake tin.

7 Slice the other banana thinly and arrange on the top of the tart. Halve the passion fruits and bash the backs with a big spoon to remove the seeds. Spread over the tart.

8 Decorate with the chocolate shavings. See the note above for tips. If you can't be bothered to do that, you could just grate with a fine grater.

£0.30 /PERSON | SERVES 20 | EASE ★★☆☆☆ | PREP 15 MINS | COOK 14 MINS | V

Pistachio Cookies

125g **softened butter**

200g **virgin coconut sugar**

1 **egg**

100g **pistachios**, chopped roughly

1 teaspoon **GF vanilla extract**

100g **ground almonds**

150g **GF self-raising flour**

1 teaspoon **xanthan gum**

1 Preheat the oven to 180°C fan oven/200°C/gas 6. Line 2 large baking trays.

2 Beat together the butter and sugar.

3 Add the egg and beat well.

4 Add the pistachios and vanilla extract and beat.

5 Add the almonds, flour and xanthan gum.

6 Turn out onto a floured board. The mixture is a little sticky, but using lightly-floured hands, form into 20 balls. Place on the baking sheets and press down lightly.

7 Bake in the oven for 14 minutes. Leave to cool.

Why virgin coconut sugar?

See page 9 to understand our approach to sugar

Vanilla Almond Cake

RON SAYS: "Technically, cocoa solids are any part of the cocoa bean in a finished chocolate. The reason we use 100% cocoa solids chocolate is to avoid any processed sugar getting into the chocolate. 100% dark chocolate has health benefits similar to fruit, vegetables and tea. All of these foods contain 'flavonoids' that have anti-oxidant and anti-inflammatory benefits."

5 **eggs**, separated

150g **virgin coconut sugar**

1 teaspoon **vanilla extract**

100g **ground almonds**

300ml **double cream**

1 tablespoon **raw honey**

100g **toasted, flaked almonds**

100% cocoa solids chocolate, to grate on top, see page 210

1 Preheat the oven to 170°C fan oven/190°C/gas 5. Grease and line a 23cm springform cake tin.

2 Beat together the egg yolks and half the coconut sugar. Add the vanilla.

3 In another bowl, beat the egg whites until they are stiff and then fold in the remaining coconut sugar and the ground almonds.

4 Gently fold the contents of both bowls together and pour into the prepared tin.

5 Bake in the oven for 25 minutes.

6 Once the cake has cooled, beat the cream, add the honey and mix together. Spread over the top, sprinkle over the almonds and grate some chocolate over the top.

Why *raw* honey?

German-Layered Pancakes

This one is great when you have friends around and you feel like making a dessert. The good thing about it is you can make most of the elements ahead of time and just assemble it at the last minute. That way you are not stuck in the kitchen for ages, when you would rather be with your guests.

Pancakes

3 **eggs**

70g **GF self-raising flour**

60g **ground almonds**

1/2 teaspoon **GF baking powder**

6 tablespoons **milk**

virgin coconut oil, to fry

Chocolate sauce

50g **butter**

100g x **100% cocoa solids chocolate**, see page 210

2 tablespoons **pure maple syrup**

4 tablespoons **double cream**

4 **oranges**

4 tablespoons **pure maple syrup**

double cream to serve

1 Mix together the pancake ingredients until smooth. Heat about a dessertspoon of the coconut oil in a small frying pan. Add 1/3 of the mixture. Allow it to spread around the pan. Cook gently on both sides until lightly browned. Repeat with the other two pancakes. Set to one side until cool.

2 To make the chocolate sauce, put the sauce ingredients in a small saucepan and gently heat until everything is melted and smooth. Set to one side to cool.

3 Cut the skins off the oranges with a sharp knife, removing all the pith. Cut three of the oranges into small segments. Cut the other one into rings to decorate the top.

4 Once everything is cooled, assemble together. Put half the small segments of orange on the bottom pancake, along with 2 tablespoons of maple syrup and a good drizzle of the chocolate sauce. Repeat with the second pancake. Put the last pancake on top and then the rings of orange on top of that, again with a couple of tablespoons of maple syrup. Drizzle the rest of the chocolate sauce on top.

5 When serving, drizzle with cream.

MAKE
YOUR
OWN

if you want to know what goes in
it...make it yourself, often easier
than you might think

Breadmaker Bread

I bought a Panasonic Breadmaker and have found it an easy way to guarantee good gluten-free bread. Here are a couple of basic recipes to use. If you don't have a breadmaker, you can find some of our bread recipes at www.noshbooks.com.

Dry ingredients

2 tablespoons **dried yeast**

360g **GF white bread flour**

1 tablespoon **GF baking powder**

2 teaspoons **xanthan gum**

1 teaspoon **salt**

Wet ingredients

270ml **warm water**, about body temperature

60g **runny raw honey**

60ml **light olive oil**

1 tablespoon **cider vinegar**

3 large (room temperature) **eggs**, beaten

1 Mix the dry ingredients together in a bowl.

2 Combine the wet ingredients and then add to the bread machine (with the GF paddle attached).

3 Add the dry ingredients to the breadmaker, don't stir.

4 Set your breadmaker going to make gluten-free bread. On the Panasonic machine it was programme 14.

5 Take the bread out of the machine as soon as the programme is finished; set an alarm so you don't miss when it finishes.

6 To make a brown, seeded loaf, just replace the white bread flour with the same amount of GF brown bread flour, together with a tablespoon each of sesame seeds, sunflower seeds and pumpkin seeds. Use exactly the same baking method.

£6.50 /500G — EASE ★☆☆☆☆ — PREP 5 MINS — V

100% Sugar-Free Chocolate

Throughout this book we suggest using 100% cocoa solids chocolate, as it contains zero processed sugar. We understand it is expensive to buy, and for that reason, we make our own. We buy our ingredients from www.healthysupplies.com. Alternatively, you can buy high percent cocoa solids chocolate, if you are not set on being completely sugar-free.

Cooking chocolate

250g **cacao butter**

125g **cacao powder**

Eating chocolate

250g **cacao butter**

125g **cacao powder**

90ml **pure maple syrup**

1 teaspoon **GF vanilla extract**

1 Simply melt the cacao butter in a small saucepan, being careful not to overheat. Take off the heat and add the cacao powder and whisk together well until smooth.

2 If you are making 'eating' chocolate, add the maple syrup and vanilla and stir well.

3 If you are making the mint chocolate from page 196, then add ½ a teaspoon of peppermint extract at stage 2.

4 Pour into either a silicon chocolate mold, or a plastic box, and leave to set. Keep stored in the fridge.

Cashew Nut Butter

We have used nut butter in quite a few recipes throughout the book. It is easy to make if you have a food processor and is much healthier than most bought nut butter.

You could replace cashews with almonds, hazelnuts or (unsalted) peanuts if you want.

400g **cashew nuts**

4 tablespoons **toasted sesame oil**

1 Put the nuts in a large frying pan and toast gently for 3-4 minutes until they are quite warm. Keep them moving to avoid scorching.

2 Place in a food processor and blitz for about 5 minutes until they form a paste. Add the oil and blitz to form a soft paste

3 Store in a glass jar with a screw top.

Waffle House Waffles

If you don't have a waffle iron, you can just fry this mixture in a frying pan. However, using a waffle iron creates a lot of surface area which gets crispy and delicious. Also, those little holes are perfect for filling with maple syrup!

Waffle irons can vary a lot. We used the highest heat setting and it worked well, but you may need to experiment with yours, to get everything nicely browned and cooked through.

Sweet waffles

300g **GF self-raising flour**

2 tablespoons **GF baking powder**

100g **virgin coconut sugar**

2 **eggs**, separated

100g **butter**, melted

500ml **milk**

Toppings

pure maple syrup

chopped hazelnuts

ice cream, see page 214 or 218

1 Put the flour, baking powder, sugar, egg yolks, melted butter and milk together in a large mixing bowl. Beat together.

2 Beat the egg whites until they are stiff. Fold gently into the batter mix.

3 Heat a waffle iron on a high heat, spray with oil and add sufficient batter to fill each pod.

4 Cook until nicely browned.

5 Serve with whatever toppings you fancy.

Coconut Sugar Vanilla Ice Cream

You can make this type of ice cream without an ice cream maker, however, this type of machine is not very expensive and it will make some of the best ice cream you will ever taste.

We keep our ice cream maker bowl in the freezer all the time, so it is always ready to go. The trick to using this machine it to make sure the bowl is totally frozen and the mixture is totally cooled before you start churning. Don't be tempted to rush.

100g **virgin coconut sugar**

4 **egg yolks**

300ml **double cream**

1/2 teaspoon **vanilla bean paste**

1 mug/300ml **milk**

1 Put the ice cream maker bowl in the freezer overnight. When you shake the bowl, you should not be able to hear the liquid moving.

2 In a bowl, beat together the sugar, egg yolks and vanilla paste.

3 Heat the milk in a small saucepan. Once the milk is almost boiling, add slowly to the egg mixture, beating while you pour.

4 Return the mixture to the pan and heat gently until the mixture thickens. Be careful not to let it overheat or the eggs will curdle.

5 Take off the heat and immediately put in a jug or bowl. Leave to cool and then put in the fridge to chill completely.

6 Slowly pour the mixture into the ice cream maker while the paddle is turning. Churn until the ice cream thickens. This could take up to 25 minutes.

7 Store in the freezer (obviously) until needed.

Why virgin coconut sugar?

See page 9 to understand our approach to sugar

One Minute Hummus

JOY SAYS: "So quick that you will never need to buy it at the supermarket again. You also know exactly what's gone into it. It's definitely the quickest recipe I have ever written!"

juice of a **lemon**

3 tablespoons **olive oil**

400g tin **chickpeas**, rinsed and drained

3 tablespoons **tahini**

salt and **pepper**

1 Whizz up all the ingredients in the blender, pop it in a jar and store in the fridge.

'Instant' Ice Cream

This is a really great way to get ice cream quickly. It differs from using an ice cream maker in that the ingredients themselves cause the ice cream to freeze and set, rather than the ice cream maker freezing the ingredients. We thought we would give you the option, in case you don't have an ice cream maker.

This can be eaten straightaway or stored in the freezer for a couple of hours before eating. Storing for any longer than that means it will freeze slightly too hard.

4 ripe **bananas**, frozen

1/2 mug/150ml **double cream**

2 tablespoons **raw honey**

1 Put the frozen bananas in the food processor and blitz. Add the cream and honey and whizz until smooth.

2 Eat!

index

REGISTER

at <u>noshbooks.com/gf</u> to get
new gluten-free recipes
emailed to you
every month

Published by: Intrade (GB) Ltd
Contact: joymay@mac.com

ISBN: 978-0-9932609-6-4

Printed in China

1st Edition: July 2018.

Author: Joy May

Design & Photography: Ben May & Tim May

Proof-reading: Fran Maciver

Editor: Ron May

Some great brands have
donated cooking gear for us
to use. Thanks so much to: